COLLECTION STRATEGIES

FOR THE

REAL ESTATE

OWNER,

LANDLORD, AND

PROPERTY MANAGER

I0437072

EULA C. DOZIER

DENVER, COLORADO

The opinions expressed in this manuscript are solely the opinions of the author and do not represent the opinions or thoughts of the publisher. The author has represented and warranted full ownership and/or legal right to publish all the materials in this book.

Collection Strategies For The Real Estate Owner, Landlord, and Property Manager
All Rights Reserved.
Copyright © 2016 Eula C. Dozier
v3.0

Cover Photo © 2016 thinkstockphotos.com. All rights reserved - used with permission.

This book may not be reproduced, transmitted, or stored in whole or in part by any means, including graphic, electronic, or mechanical without the express written consent of the publisher except in the case of brief quotations embodied in critical articles and reviews.

Outskirts Press, Inc.
http://www.outskirtspress.com

ISBN: 978-1-4787-6391-8

Outskirts Press and the "OP" logo are trademarks belonging to Outskirts Press, Inc.

PRINTED IN THE UNITED STATES OF AMERICA

TABLE OF CONTENTS

FOREWORD

This book has been created because I have seen a great need.

<u>FIRST</u>, this need is for the beginning investors as well as the experienced ones. I have talked to many people, some who had already started their investment careers, some with substantial holdings, and people who were only thinking of investing. They all had many different worries, but the one that surfaced most concerned tenants. Heading the list of tenant problems was "How do I collect the rents from the tenant?" and "what will I do if the tenant won't pay me?" Well, I know the answer to these questions, you see, I was a Professional Collector for over 15 years. I started investing in Real Estate after reading my first "How To" book and it took me less than five years to acquire enough Real Estate to match my salary. Thus, I could retire before I reached my 40th birthday.

To tell you the truth, I feel as though I've been "set free", I get motivated just thinking about what Real Estate has done for me, and every time I hear someone mention it, I join right in the conversation. I start to tell the story of how I was working a full-time job and managing over 30 units with no delinquent rents, and very few vacancies. After hearing my story, many of the people use to ask for my advice.

My mother heard me explaining some Real Estate ideas to a person one day, and she said "you ought to write that down", so I started to jot things down when people would ask me a question. That's how I know that the information in this book is what Real Estate investors need to know. My mother and other people felt that I had a workable system and valuable knowledge that needed to be shared with other struggling investors. It was a very small task for me to write down the "System" in a step-by-step format, because I was using it then, I'm still using it today, and it was first produced in 1987. All opinions, findings, conclusions, and recommendations expressed in this book are practical and have been used by the author.

SECONDLY, these times we live in are crucial times, and there has been no greater time in recent history when we need to stress "Cash Flow". Many times new laws are passed, some favorable, some unfavorable, but smart investors know that "Cash Flow" is the answer, the new rule to accumulating wealth. Within the pages of this book, I will show you how to collect the rent, which is the primary method of achieving wealth through Real Estate today. I will show you the secrets that I was forced to learn, which can mean the difference between success and failure for you.

Whereas the author does not claim to provide any legal, accounting, or any other professional services, this book is designed to give accurate instructional information concerning collections.

THIRDLY, I wrote this book because of my own self-gratification. I have a personal goal of helping people who are willing to put their capital at risk and invest in Real Estate. With the details that I've set down in this book, rent collections should become almost automatic. This book is easy to read and follow. It makes me feel good inside to know that I've given you a proven "System", and all you have to do, is follow it. When you have finished reading this book, you will be equipped to deal with your Real Estate holdings and collect your rents!

1
INTRODUCTION

COLLECTION STRATEGIES FOR THE REAL ESTATE OWNER,
LANDLORD, AND PROPERTY MANAGER.

Tenant Problems Hold Real Estate Investors Back.

I write this book for those of you who are planning to go into real estate, the beginner investor who has already purchased a few properties and the old timers as well. Just as important as the innovative new ideas and techniques to purchase real estate, is the know how to make the endeavor profitable.

The major reason people do not buy more real estate is tenant problems. They are afraid; they would be "Certifiable" if they weren't. They don't know how to properly select, collect from, or evict a tenant. These people seem to know about many of the problems that a landlord has. They seem to know that you can very easily come by an "unplanned Negative Cash Flow" without a proper system to work by.

In trying times (and you'll have some), this book will instruct you to act logically, rather than react emotionally. You will also find the forms and the instructions on how to easily keep the appropriate records for tax time, and to assure that you are indeed making a profit.

There are many good tenants out there, and I've found that when the rent is paid, most tenants seem to be much happier. Unfortunately for the landlord, some turn into Oscar the Grouch when they are behind in the rent. A tenant may not perceive the changes in their state of mind, but the landlord will be extremely aware, by the tenant's actions and attitude.

It would be best for a landlord to formulate a plan to "educate the tenant" and "collect the rent when it's due", so the both of you can be happier going forward. This will be a reality, because I solve the problems of how to select, collect from, and evict a tenant in this book.

Some People Need Permission.

Some people hold themselves back. For one reason or another they think they cannot do what others have done, they do not feel themselves worthy, and they ultimately will not give themselves permission to be successful.

The Wizard of Oz was right. Most of the successful people (Real Estate collectors in this case) of the world are no better than the average person, but they have something that the average person may not have, and that something is the "permission" to be successful. That problem will be resolved right now, there is a poster (page 100) bestowing upon you the permission to become successful. All you have to do is to read it and believe it.

When you have read this book completely, you will find, a well-deserved "Certificate of Achievement" (page 120). This Certificate is suitable for framing and should be a source of pride and inspiration to you. You should type in your name, and the date to complete it.

Hopefully, in combination with the knowledge you are about to receive from this book, the Certificate of Achievement, and the Permission Poster, you too, will strive to become successful.

The Wise Investor Collects.

You must know how to plan, keep records, and collect your

rents. There are numerous programs and systems out there to get rich through real estate, and most of them will work at least in the first phases of acquiring the property. BUT, getting rich or making a substantial profit through the purchase of real estate is not the same as just making a purchase for tax shelter or buying and waiting years for property appreciation before selling. Now days, with the new tax laws, and in some places rent controls, you must be a wise investor to make a profit.

There are scores of speculators meeting financial ruin from common mistakes associated with the purchase, maintenance, and control of real estate. My area of concentration and the focus of this book is the control part, which is scheduling the rent rolls, forms used for month-to-month tenancy, leases, and evictions. The collection of rents will be covered in detail later on, because even if you made the best real estate purchase deal of the Century, you would still find yourself in trouble if the rents were not being collected properly.

I feel this is a teachable moment. I am also a Computer Instructor and when I want to get an important point across, I tell the students what I'm about to tell them, I tell them, and then I tell them what I told them. Look for it in this book and remember, collecting rents is best done when "the rent first becomes due" and "the tenant is still in your apartment".

I have prepared an effective step-by-step method of collecting the rent every month when followed correctly. It would be a good idea to have a pencil handy while reading this book. I have included a "Notes" page at the end of each chapter, so that you may jot down any notes, reactions, and ideas you have about the chapter. The "Notes" page provides a central location for your own responses, which will hopefully motivate and inspire you. It will be a reminder as to where exactly to find useful information quickly. It should remind you of what success can do for you, and move you on toward your goal.

Most of the information presented in this book will be done based on two assumptions: (1) that the reader has already purchased the property; and (2) that the general condition of that property is good. Many books are already on the market about "how to purchase Real Estate", "how to be a Contractor", Nothing Down", and so forth, but my focus here, however, is the "How To" of where the profit comes in. The basics to successful Property Management are, make all the necessary repairs, choose the right tenants, and collect all the rents.

The Property Must Be Properly Maintained.

Often, the beginning investor starts out by purchasing a "fix-a-up-per". Since most of these houses are in poor condition, your money, your time, and/or your labor must be allocated for repairs. When I say repairs, I don't mean the "Band-Aid" method. I mean fixing what needs to be fixed. If you know what needs to be repaired before you make the purchase, there will be few surprises. If you need a whole new roof, plan to replace the entire roof. You could patch it up (and I've done it), but you may find as I did, that it increases your problems, and eventually could cost you more money in the long run. You might feel that you can get around fixing it up by lowering the rent, but only the most undesirable of tenants would want it, and besides the City Inspectors will be on your back. Local municipalities can legally condemn a building for certain violations, so go ahead and fix it up right.

No matter how good or bad tenants are, they will complain, and with good reason, if their drapes, sofa, bed, and TV are being soaked when it rains. A law suit against you would be justified, and you don't need that. The tenant's motto is "All's fair in Love, War, and any Dispute they have with a landlord". You get the idea.... Fix it up from the start!

The "fix-a-upper" is probably a good idea for the beginning investor from the standpoint that it's cheap, which is many times all the beginner can afford. Assuming the beginner makes the necessary repairs, there is another problem. What quality of tenant will the property attract?

You will learn how to handle these tenants and their responsibilities. You will learn methods of rent collections, eviction procedures, and some remedies for potential problems before they arise.

The Real Estate Concept Fails Without Rent Collections.

Unless you plan to buy, renovate, and sell real estate for a profit within the very same month, you will undoubtedly at some point in time find yourself involved in renting an apartment or house and trying to collect the rent. A tenant could be occupying the property when you purchase it. Either way you see, without the rent, the whole real estate concept fails. It's simple; the rent is part of your income. You collect the rent and you make a profit. If you don't, you have to pay the mortgage, taxes, water bill, repairs, insurance, etc. out of your own pocket, and the tenant can live in your property for free. So then, you have a few choices; (1) let the tenant stay for free, (2) learn to collect the rent yourself, (3) hire a property management company to collect it for you, (4) sell the property, (5) evict the tenants if you can, (6) or any combination of the above.

I personally know of a landlord who could not collect the rents so he would not make any repairs to the property, and he stopped paying the water bill and the taxes. He owned the house free and clear so he thought he would just wait the tenants out. At first glance, it would appear no harm, but over a period of about two years the property was in such a run-down condition that he had property violations and did not have the money to fix it up. To add to his problems, the city started foreclosure for less than $5,000.00 past due taxes and water bills. He experienced a rude awakening as he could not borrow the money due to a poor credit rating. The end result was that he lost his property to the city.

The most ideal situation of owning a property free and clear turned out to be a nightmare for him because he did not know how to collect the rent, or what course of action to follow when he was not being paid. There is a lesson to be learned here. It is simply this, if you plan to own real estate, plan to collect the rent, or quickly follow the correct legal procedure for eviction.

This one factor of rent collection is the most disastrous mistake a real estate owner could make. You could be making a disastrous mistake if you start to think "well, I'll give this tenant a chance to get on his feet", or "I'll make sure to collect the rent next month", or "I'm too busy working on my next deal to worry about that now". All I will say here is re-think the situation because that's a lick on you! Nobody ever made a profit by losing money.

Real Estate Is A Business.

Some people are very uncomfortable asking for money and feel that it's something personal. Remember, however, it is a business, and you are only doing your job. Contrary to what you might have heard, you don't need to be "hard hearted" to be a good collector, just be of average intelligence, have a set goal, and get motivated to do what you have to do.

There is no middle of the road if you own rental property. The decision to collect must be made (not just a period, but exclamation point)! The tenant is not your pal, and don't become too well-acquainted because it will seem personal when you collect rent. You will start to feel that you are charging too much rent, you'll begin to over repair, and furnish things that are not in your budget like a Ceiling Fan, a new sliding window for the kitchen, etc. It is not always easy, but sometimes you might even have to say "no". Explain to the tenant that larger repair budgets translate into increased rental charges.

When tenants continue to ask for things, I have given them a piece of paper and asked them to write down everything they want so I can accurately figure out what the new rental amount will be. I let them know I can get marble floors, a swimming pool, and even a gold toilet if they want it, but it's going to cost. It's amazing how tenants can't think of a thing that they want when confronted with this scenario.

Be yourself, give respect, and demand it in return. You can be business-like and polite, but you have to be firm. You have to collect the rent; you have to "step up to the pump". Through the next few chapters in this book, knowledge and success are yours.

No Wish To Offend Readers.

I would like to apologize to anyone who sees this as me maliciously attacking someone personally, or ragging on this group that I call tenants because the book may be a little harsh, but it's not my intent, and I use to be a tenant myself. Whereas I do not wish to offend, and I only intend to convey truth; I feel that I'm require to explain that all the comments and suggestions in this book is not the modus operandi of every tenant. In fact it may only be a small number that may cause these problems, but that small number of tenants is the biggest factor that could cause an unknowing landlord to suffer loss.

Sometimes I might inject humor or give an account of imaginary or real people and events, to get the point across. You might find expressions that draw your attention, words that convey information and instructions, but realize that the facts provided are not meant to be harmful or mean-spirited toward anybody.

I believe that the information provided in this book will be very helpful to some landlords caught in certain situations. I only wish I had this information when I first got started. And because I understand that "God is my source", I'm not trying to be more that I am, I'm humbly presenting this information for those who need it. Also please forgive for any overlooked items, mistakes, misspellings, or misprints that might have occurred.

NOTE$

_____

_____

_____

_____

_____

_____

_____

_____

_____

_____

_____

_____

_____

_____

_____

_____

_____

_____

_____

CHAPTER I

2
SEE THE WHOLE PICTURE

*COLLECTION STRATEGIES FOR THE REAL ESTATE OWNER,
LANDLORD, AND PROPERTY MANAGER.*

Be Aware Of Expenses.

If you are in the process of buying or have just purchased one of
the many wonderful real estate "How to make a Million" books or
courses, beware of understated and left out costs and expenses. Don't
let anyone tell you that there are only a few expenses. Some of these
books only mention Mortgage payments, taxes, and insurance, but in
addition, there are substantial other costs that you might have to shell
out bucks for such as water, gas, electricity, stationary, envelopes,
pens, pencils, stamps, telephone bills, advertising fees, attorney, closing cost, marshal, court fees, transportation and parking, etc. The list
goes on.... Not to mention your own time and efforts which could be
extensive, for which you should be compensated.

Plan For Expenses.

I strongly advise that you plan, and plan well. You should save at
least 10% of one month's rental income each month for a rainy day.
Why? Let's consider some hypothetical situations. What happens if
the tenant calls one night when it's freezing out and says the furnace

has just quit? What happens if the tenant moves out in the middle of the night and you not only didn't get the rent, but you now have to pay for the gas, electric, and water he used? What happens if you discover damage (holes in the walls, torn linoleum on the kitchen floor, or possible a broken window)? Another consideration is what if the tenant got confused when he moved out that night and took the brand new appliances you had just installed? You must be prepared to deal with these "what if" situations and that 10% should cover most of them. Insurance may cover some problems, but start putting in too many claims, and your premium is sure to go up as well.

I don't want to scare you away from real estate investing because it is truly a great wealth builder, but it comes with big responsibilities and potential problems. The problems can be minimized, however, if handled properly. To do so, you must be aware of the many pitfalls and always collect the rents when due.....you will need them.

Gather Your Courage.

I have to attest to the fact that it truly takes courage to stick your neck out far enough to purchase income property. Fear of the unknown will always be there, but the person with enough self-confidence can overcome it. To get the necessary confidence, you must have knowledge.

I will share with you a few of my own experiences here just to let you know it can be done. Needless to say, purchasing that first property was one of the hardest things that I have ever done. It "scared the socks off me". Signing that first contract was a hair-raising experience, and I believe that this is another major reason why more people do not get involved in Real Estate. I used to wake up in the middle of the night, get out of my bed, get fully dressed, and take a ride all the way across town just to make sure the property was still there.

Make The First Deal "A GOOD DEAL".

Here's what happened. After reading my first Real Estate "How

To" book, I had about $5,000.00 saved and went out looking. I went by the 100 house rule at that time, and I looked at over 100 houses before I made my first offer. This was a good idea in my case because I didn't know anything about Real Estate. I got used to the market, and I finally began to understand the pricing of housing in my area. You have to know something about price, why one house on the other side or down the street is worth more than that house. Compare and school yourself on different amenities. You have to know about why the value is different in different neighborhoods.

When I was ready, and after much negotiating, I managed to purchase a two-family house, 3-bedrooms each side, 6-by-6. I persuaded the owner (who owned it free and clear) to hold a 10 year, 10% mortgage. This was a very low down payment deal, and the monthly payments were not bad either. The house was in fair condition. For fix-up I spent approximately $2,000.00 for materials. I replaced some broken windows, as well as exterior doors and locks, installed storm doors, and did some badly need interior painting. My brother Kenneth and I performed all the labor involved. The mortgage payments were low, and the rent for each apartment was slightly raised, so everything was working out fine.

After I paid the taxes, insurance, water, and miscellaneous expenses, I still had a healthy cash flow each month. I put over $200.00 a month into my pocket. I made this a goal, to make at least $200.00 a month on each property I purchased.

Approximately three years later I sold that property for a lot more than I paid for it. In that short time I was shocked to find that mortgage reduction had taken place and I owed a lot less for the total pay out to the mortgage holder. I discovered that the tenants had paid off over $2,000.00 of my current mortgage balance! What a deal, in such a short time. At closing, I walked away with approximately $24,000.00, this after all the closing cost and completely paying off that first mortgage. After following that whole cycle, it did not take me very long to figure out that Real Estate was for me! This is when I first understood that instead of working hard for the money, that I was able to let the money work hard for me.

Look for "No" or "Low" Down Payment Deals.

I remember my first "nothing down" deal. One year when I was still employed at GMAC, I owned a 1977 Buick that was nearly paid for. I found a two-family, 3-bedroom up and 2-bedroom down, that I could not pass up. I persuaded this owner to hold a mortgage also, but we had one problem; I didn't want to part with the down payment money. After thinking about it for some time, I decided to re-finance the car for the $2,000.00 down payment.

I felt that the most significant thing about this deal was that I had it all worked out so that I personally never had one cent invested in the deal, and I never had to make another payment on my car. I borrowed money on the car to buy the house, and then I let the house pay for the car. I had a small cash flow each month even after paying all the expenses, the mortgage, and the car payment.

I raised the rent about a year later and my cash flow grew. After 24 months when the car was paid off, I found another advantage; my cash flow grew even more.

Look For Bargain Buys.

Sometime later, I encountered a gentleman with a VA mortgage who had filed Bankruptcy. He only wanted $1,000.00 for his equity. There was only one stipulation that I had to meet, and that was to purchase the dining room set that was still sitting in the property. He didn't have anywhere to put the set, and he felt it was too good to just throw away.

He wanted $500.00 for the whole dining room set, and I gave him $1,500.00 cash. I assumed an $8,000.00 VA mortgage on this 3 Bedroom, single family house. After a few years, with a little fix-up, the house appraised at over $50,000.00.

Be Persistent And Visualize Success.

Each purchase is a whole new experience. Sometimes it may take a while to get an offer accepted, but it will happen if you keep working at it long enough. In approximately five years, I became financially independent of my 9-to-5 job, and I believe anybody can.

It takes guts! One person I know, quit his job, and pursued his own real estate entrepreneurship, after acquiring only three properties. He brought his papers to my house; we put it on the table. He showed me his profits from the properties after expenses. He told me his wife was working and laid out her salary and their household expenses. After our discussion, I truly could not say that he couldn't do what he was planning.

I had purchased a total of about 17 separate properties (one, two, and three family units), and each was yielding me a profit of $200.00 to $600.00 per month cash flow (some substantially more), before I made my move.

It may seem somewhat discouraging as you read about all of the problems covered in this book, but if you stand back and think about it, you will be able to see the advantages too. It's worth it! Absorbing the knowledge contained herein is necessary for you to gain the power and capability of addressing the problems as they arise. Just visualize the success that comes if you put forth the energy to control your own destiny. "The quality of your future life style will be a direct result of your efforts today". Go for it. Set a goal, and remember that Real Estate makes millionaires.

NOTE$

_____

_____

_____

_____

_____

_____

_____

_____

_____

_____

_____

_____

_____

_____

_____

_____

_____

_____

_____

_____

CHAPTER 2

3

MAINTENANCE, UPKEEP, AND ASSOCIATED BILLS

COLLECTION STRATEGIES FOR THE REAL ESTATE OWNER,
LANDLORD, AND PROPERTY MANAGER.

Owners Responsibilities.

The first thing I would like to do in this section is give you some of your basic responsibilities as the owner and landlord. These things may vary in different parts of the country, but I would look at these closely no matter where you stay. The property must be kept sanitary, free of any health or safety hazards. The following is a list of the most commonly noted violations.

- presence of dirt, rodents, or insects. (unless caused by the tenant)
- lack of sufficient heat or hot water. (most laws require that you maintain a furnace capable of producing 68 degrees heat in all living areas)
- leaking roof
- crumbling plaster
- weak, sagging floors

- lead paint
- cluttered, unsafe stairs or exits
- electrical problems such as faulty wiring or inadequate lighting
- plumbing problems

The basic responsibility for maintaining the apartment free of health and safety hazards cannot be transferred from the landlord to the tenant. If the lease states that the tenant is responsible for repairing any of the before mentioned conditions, that clause of the lease may be unenforceable.

Even if you have a month-to-month rental agreement, I strongly advise against allowing a tenant to work on your property in lieu of rent payments. Some tenants will even try to convince you that they are expert roofers, plumbers, and painters, but all too often, they are not. If the repairs are not done or improperly done, you are worse off than when you started. You could have flushed the money that you spent for those wasted materials. You are yet responsible for those repairs; you didn't get any rent for that period of time, and on top of all that, you still may have to evict to be rid of this tenant.

Your obligation to provide a safe, clean environment is not suspended even if the tenant owes you rent. Later, we will discuss what you should do if the tenant will not pay, but make sure that you always take care of your obligations. I must warn you, repairs never get cheaper if you wait. As a matter of fact, the longer you wait, the greater the odds for worse damage, higher associated costs, and tenant dissatisfaction.

Advertising Sources.

Now, let's talk advertising for a minute. In order to attract as many potential tenants as possible, you should take advantage of a variety of advertising sources.

Besides placing an expensive "want ad" in the local newspaper, there are other means you should consider to publicize your vacancy.

Some Realtors, city or town agencies, and social services departments offer a free registry services for landlords, which provides information on available apartments to hundreds of prospective tenants each month.

Other possibilities include advertising your apartment in neighborhood papers, posting the information on bulletin boards in supermarkets, laundromats, and other stores in your area, or working through the housing offices of local colleges.

If you choose to engage one of the professional listing agents or companies which advertise regularly, you should make certain you find out, in advance, what fees you will be charged and exactly what services you will be provided for your money.

Utility Cost.

Escalating energy costs are a burden to everyone. If the arrangement with your tenant is that utilities are to be included in his or her rent (that is, you pay the utility costs), you will naturally want to keep the bills as low as possible. You can do this and still satisfy your legal responsibility to provide the tenant with adequate heat and electricity, by making sure that the apartment is well "weatherized".

There are a number of different programs to help you insulate, weather-strip, caulk, upgrade your furnace, and make other energy-saving improvements to your property. These programs include counseling on energy conservation, loans or grants for materials, and in some cases, free labor. They are administered by various government and social agencies, as well as your local Gas and Electric Company.

Even if your tenant pays his or her own utility bills, you may find that it is advantageous for you to be sure that the building is energy efficient. Manageable utility costs will help keep a tenant from being delinquent in paying the rent and sometimes spare you the expense of pursuing an eviction.

Go For Separate Utilities When Possible.

There are two other good reasons why I do not pay for the tenant's heat, anymore! First, the tenants feel that there is no reason to conserve because their heat allowance is included in the rent and the rent remains constant, whether the heat is one dollar or one hundred dollars. Secondly, there is less wear and tear on the furnace when the thermostat is kept at a reasonable temperature. In other words, if tenants have to pay for their own heat they will try to save their own money, and thereby put less strain on your furnace.

Once I was supplying heat for a two family house that I was renting out. The bill got bigger and bigger as the winter months came. Even though the apartment was well insulated, I knew something was wrong. One day in mid-winter, with an approximate 25 degree temperature, I stopped by the property to collect the rent. As I approached the house I noticed that the living room windows to the front apartment were open. When I went inside, I asked the tenant why the windows were open when it was freezing outside. His answer was "it's hot in here! ! !"

Even though the thermostat was in this tenant's apartment, he made the decision to open the windows when it became too hot, rather than walk over and adjust the thermostat. At that point, I realized there were some things that had to change. First; the tenant really didn't have anything to loose, and Secondly; I had actually given him the right to do what he was doing.

Needless to say, I had a new meter set, separated the electric, put in another furnace, another water heater, put a thermostat in both apartments, and dropped the rent by a minimal amount on each. This means each apartment's energy use was measured, and each tenant had to pay for their own consumption. I think I can truthfully say that I cured that problem of wasted energy because thereafter, I noticed that the windows were always closed in the winter.

Help For Financing Repairs.

If you cannot afford to fix up your property there are a number of programs run by the federal, state, city, and county governments to help landlords pay for needed repairs on their properties. These programs vary as to their income requirements, neighborhoods covered, and the amount of funds available.

You can find out whether you are eligible for one of these programs by calling your local office of Neighborhood Rehabilitation Services if they are available in your area. If you own in a suburban area, you may qualify for a community development grant to help repair your property. Your local Town Hall representative can give you more information about the available programs.

There are some exceptions in towns that have established their own offices to administer community development programs. Contact with these offices can also be made by calling the Town Hall or Village Office.

The "SECTION 8" Program.

Many landlords have found that participation in the "Section 8 Housing Assistance Payments Program" allows them to collect a substantial rent for their apartments while keeping tenant turnover low.

Designed to help low to moderate income families and senior citizens afford decent housing, this federal program can pay a large portion of the tenant's rent subsidy directly to the landlord. Renters who qualify for this program pay between 15 to 25 percent of their monthly income toward the rent. The difference between what they pay and the actual rent, is paid to the landlord by a grant, administered by your local Housing Authority.

In order for your property to qualify to be rented under Section 8 guidelines, it must not rent for more than the current "fair market rents". These rent levels are set by the federal government and include all utilities. If your rental arrangement is set up so that the tenant pays utilities, adjustments will be made.

NOTE$

_____

_____

_____

_____

_____

_____

_____

_____

_____

_____

_____

_____

_____

_____

_____

_____

_____

_____

_____

_____

CHAPTER 3

4
HOW TO PLAN YOUR PROFITS

COLLECTION STRATEGIES FOR THE REAL ESTATE OWNER,
LANDLORD, AND PROPERTY MANAGER.

Is There A Profit.

In the two succeeding chapters we went over things like expenses, maintenance, and how to save money, but now we will determine whether or not you are making a profit. I am not referring to the profit you could see if you sell the property over the next few years should the value of the property increase. I am not referring to the paper entry of depreciation, which allows you a tax write-off. Rather, I am referring to the profit you should see monthly.... a cold, hard, cash profit from the rents you'll be receiving each month.

You should make an analysis before purchasing income property to insure a profit. Remember, this book will not provide you with all the information you need to purchase real estate, but you will be able to recognize the presence or absence of a profit. We will be discussing mortgage payments, and you may need an amortization book to determine your own payment amounts. If your mortgage payments are made to the bank or a mortgage broker, the taxes and insurance are usually included in the payments. This is referred to as PITI- principal, interest, taxes, and insurance. In our examples, they will be separate.

Forms To Keep Your Records.

There are three simple forms that we will look at, two in this chapter and one in the next. They were devised to determine if there is a profit to be had, and to help you keep your records straight all year long. When forms are created, the most important thing is focusing on the purpose of the form in order to develop it more effectively. Note: if you have a computer you will be able to keep records there using programs such as QuickBooks or something similar.

Forms can be used as a vehicle for collecting and presenting information. There are many important advantages to this uniformity. It is easy to see if the information is complete and accurate on a form, even if many different people must complete it. The sequence, the questions, the providing of simple instructions, and prompts will help to guide the person completing the form.

If you have need of a form, create one. It will greatly reduce the amount of time and effort required to provide information. A list of common choices can be printed on a form to be circled or checked. Frequently used phrases and words can be printed on the form to limit the amount of writing necessary. For some people, the visual representation of a form is in itself a helpful guide, especially when important areas and key words on the form are highlighted. Remember, a simple form can not only store a great deal of information, it can be easily filed as well. Let's take a brief look at some of the forms you may find helpful.

Property Analysis Form.

The first form is the "PROPERTY ANALYSIS", see page 101. This form is designed to make it easy to get and keep all the facts and figures that you need in one place. Notice that I listed the Assessor's Office first, because that's where you call to get much of your initial information such as the name and address of the owner of record, the assessed value, and the tax number of the property you intend to purchase. Needless to say, when you find out the owners name, be certain you are talking to the right person or the agent of the right person in your negotiations. If the name of the person who's trying to sell the property, and the name of the person listed on the assessor's records are different, you should immediately find out why.

You might find that there are other owners on record that might not have been mentioned who will also have to be dealt with because they have a financial interest in the property. As for the assessed value, you can compare it to the asking price and ask questions if there's a big difference. You will possibly need the tax number of the property in order to get the figures from the City and County.

When you call the City Tax office, you may find that they break your taxes down into four categories, (1) Property Tax, (2) School Tax, (3) Embellishment, and (4) Refuse Collection. All these are listed on the right side of the form, but their total is to be posted in the City Tax column on the left side of the form. The City Taxes can usually be paid in three or four separate installments.

Often the County taxes will be one sum, but in some places can be paid in two or three separate installments. Ask plenty of questions about the taxes, the current owner of record may be eligible for some discount such as for age, or some other advantages like a Homestead reduction, that you might not qualify for.

The two water columns can be filled out by calling your local water bureau and the pure waters office for an exact amount of water consumption billed the previous year. If you can't do that, then the "rule of thumb" figure that I use in my area is $15.00 per month for each apartment. In other words, if this is a 3 family dwelling, I recommend posting $45.00 per month, which equals $540.00 a year which you would be allocating for water expenses. Some people feel that $10.00 per month is sufficient, but in this part of New York I would say that $15.00 is closer to being accurate. It all depends on how many gallons of water your tenant uses, and the amount you have to pay per gallon. To find out what "rule of thumb" figure what works best in your area, pick at random separate water bills to six separate living units, find out the amounts for the previous year and total them. Now, divide that number by six for the average amount per year; then divide by 12 for the average amount per month. The resulting figure is the one you should use.

The City Refuse column is there just in case the refuse was not included on the City Tax bill. In this part of New York, if a property is a one to three family dwelling, it is considered a Residential Property and the refuse is billed in the City Tax. On the other hand, if it is a dwelling with four or more families it is considered commercial in nature. This means you would have to employ one of the private refuse collection services at your expense, and would use this column. By the way, commercial properties are also taxed at a higher rate.

The sum of the city tax, county tax, water, and refuse collection fees per year should give you a good idea of what the expenses will be. If you divide this by twelve you will have approximately one month's expense. Keep in mind that you are only trying to get your own list of expenses to compare with that of the seller's at this point, and yet you have not included any repairs that may need to be done.

Always call the zoning office in your area to make sure that the property is legally zoned for what the seller has it listed. What I mean is that the property may be sold to you as a three family dwelling, but only zoned as a two family dwelling. The owner could have divided one of the apartments in order to get additional rent. In some places, this is a serious offense. The owner caught operating this way could be fined and/or jailed. Do not think that you can just go down to the zoning office and get it changed later, because there are strict laws concerning the use of residential property which sometimes consider, living space per tenant, the zoning of the particular neighborhood, the number of doors and exits, the lot size that the property sits on, etc.

I have included the Delinquent Bills section so that while you are talking to the city, county, or water office, you can jot down any outstanding overdue bills. Any present unpaid bills should be mentioned to your attorney. Ensure they are paid before you close on the property or at the time of closing.

Use the comments section when you are talking to the seller or anyone else about the property. It would be helpful to write down anything that is important, something you want to find out more about, or a question you may wish to ask. As I fore-stated, you should maintain good information about the property in one place, along with any notes that you might want to make.

Fixed Expenses Form.

The second form called "FIXED EXPENSES" is used all during the year as you pay the bills, and should be kept in the front of your portfolio folder. If you update this form as required, you will be very happy when tax time comes around because you will have your insurance, taxes, and water bills right at hand, as well as the dates you paid them, and your check numbers, all in one place. Accountants like to see that; they think you're organized. The form is self-explanatory. See page 102.

You might notice an item listed on the form called "C of O", which stands for Certificate of Occupancy. This Certificate is required before a landlord can legally rent an apartment in this part of New York. When you apply for a "C of O" at City Hall, a City Inspector will make an appointment with the landlord to inspect the property for Health and Safety issues. If violations are found, the landlord is notified and given time to fix whatever repairs are needed.

Use These Forms.

If you already own property, I suggest you take this opportunity to complete one of the above-mentioned forms for each of your properties. You may discover something you did not know before. This is also a good time to re-evaluate each of your properties and consider whether increasing the rents would be feasible. If you have a lease with your tenant, you cannot increase the rent until the term of the lease expires. There is an exception to this rule that occurs when the lease contains an escalation clause, which would give you the right to increase the rent.

Without a lease, you may increase the rent by giving notice to the tenant at least 30 days before the next rent payment is due. No shorter notice is valid unless the tenant pays rent in shorter intervals. That is, if the rent is paid on a weekly basis, one weeks' notice should be sufficient.

Where there are no rent controls in effect, you may increase the rent as much as you wish, providing you give your tenant proper notice. You should bear in mind, of course, that tenants will not continue to live in a place which is severely overpriced. The end result may be a turnover problem and/or a property that is very hard to rent. Although the law does not specify that notice of a rent increase must be written, it is always wise to put all such notices in writing.

A Word About Checks.

If you accept checks, make the deposit right away, or if you feel that there may be a problem, go directly to the tenants bank and get the cash, and deposit it into your account. Another thing to watch out for is a check drawn on out-of-town banks, because it will take from 5 to 10 days for you to find out if it bounces. You can always call the bank to see if the check is good, or you can demand cash from the tenant if you think he's trying to trick you.

NOTE$

_____

_____

_____

_____

_____

_____

_____

_____

_____

_____

_____

_____

_____

_____

_____

_____

_____

_____

_____

_____

_____

_____

CHAPTER 4

5

CASH FLOW STATISTIC

COLLECTION STRATEGIES FOR THE REAL ESTATE OWNER, LANDLORD, AND PROPERTY MANAGER.

Cash Flow Statistic Form.

In the preceding chapter we established the importance of forms and their proper usage. Several forms were discussed but there is yet another that this writer considers so important that this entire chapter is dedicated to it. To more effectively explain the use of this form, we will walk through a real estate deal at the same time.

This form is the "CASH FLOW STATISTIC". It breaks down income and expenses by the month. It also allows you to calculate up to three offers, compare them, and then chooses the one you feel will be accepted by the seller. This form is self-explanatory and should be completed for each property. We will examine the form section by section, and learn how to structure a real estate offer. Now, before we go on, look at the entire form on page 103.

Property Information Section.

PROPERTY ADDRESS ___55 Buyme St.___	AGENT ___Eager Realty Co.___
OWNER'S NAME ___John B. Seller___	ADDRESS ___2 Sundown La.___
OWNER'S ADDRESS ___1000 Turnover Place___	PHONE # ___222-2222___
OWNER'S PHONE # ___333-3333___	MORTGAGE BALANCE $ ___$35,000.00___
MORTGAGE HOLDER ___Mr. Outatown Inc.___	MONTHLY PAYMENT $ ___$394.91___
ASKING PRICE $ ___$60,000.00___	MORTGAGE ASSUMABLE YES / NO
	CIRCLE ONE

SECTION 1. The PROPERTY INFORMATION section is located at the top of the form. There is a space for the property address, the owners name, address, and phone number; the Real Estate Agents name, and phone number; the asking price, the mortgage balance, the mortgage holders name, and the monthly payment. Circle yes if the existing mortgage is assumable or no if it is not. Keep in mind this mortgage could be held by another individual, and some time you can assume if your credit is good.

The reason I consider this section so valuable is because once I made an extremely reasonable offer for a property before I developed this form. The person I met at the property said he would look over my offer and get back to me. I talked to him maybe twice more over the course of the next month. I found later that the property was sold on an offer submitted after the one I made, and for a lesser amount. How could this happen? The person I met at the property was only the maintenance man; the owner lived in Canada. The maintenance man probably was keeping my offer from the owner in favor of his own job security, that's when I made it a point to know who the owner is and negotiate with him.

Income Information Section.

Section 2. (Income Information) /

	CURRENT RENT	LOCATION AND BEDROOMS	PROJECTED RENT
Apt # 1.	$ 355.00	2 Bedroom - Up	$ 355.00
Apt # 2.	$ 425.00	2 Bedroom - Front	$ 425.00
Apt # 3.	$ 345.00	2 Bedroom - Rear	$ 345.00
Apt # 4.	$		$
TOTAL INCOME	$ 1,125.00		$ 1,125.00

SECTION 2. This section indicates the amount of rent generated by the property. I have modified the form to accommodate up to four apartments. Post the amount of rent the owners is now getting per month for each apartment or, if the apartment is empty, indicate the amount that the owner feels he could get, in the "CURRENT RENTS" column.

The "PROJECTED RENTS" column is for the amount for which you feel you can reasonably expect to rent the apartment for. In other words, if the high rent paying tenant currently in the apartment moved out, would you be able to rent the apartment for at least the same amount to another tenant? If not, then utilize this column, as being fact when calculating your income and expenses. From these rents you will have to pay all the bills and make repairs, so make sure they are realistic. If you see any apartment in the building that is renting for more than the average in your area, it is time to ask questions. It is not unheard of, for a seller to over-state income and/or understate expenses to make the property show a false cash flow.

Now write in the number of bedrooms for each apartment and where it is located (up, down, side, rear, etc.). The monthly rents taken in by the apartment in our example, total $1,125.00. You can see that the CURRENT RENTS and the PROJECTED RENTS agree. Multiply by twelve to get the yearly income. This is one of the most important factors in the purchase.

Offer Information.

1. $ 60,000 $ 10,000 $ 15,000   at 12 % for 25 years = $ 157,99   per month
2. $ 65,000 $ 10,000 $ 17,000   at 8 % for 25 years = $ 131.21   per month
3. $_____ $ _____ $_____   at __ % for __ years = $_____   per month

SECTION 3 pertains to the purchase offer you intend to make to the seller. You already know what the asking price is, and you have seen the property by now, so you want to make an offer that will be acceptable to the seller, while at the same time advantageous to yourself. You can structure as many as three offers and compare them to each other.

The "total amount of your offer" that you want the seller to accept goes into the OFFER column.

Your DOWN payment is self-explanatory. This is the amount of money you intend to pay at closing.

OWNER MORTGAGE is the amount which you hope the seller will finance for you.

NOTE: The sum of the BALANCE DUE on the first mortgage, your DOWN payment, and the OWNER MORTGAGE will equal your OFFER amount. For example, in our fictitious real estate deal, the ASKING PRICE is $60,000.00, and the BALANCE DUE on the first mortgage is $35,000.00 which we want to assume (or go for new money). Let us suppose that we are going to offer the full price with $10,000.00 DOWN, and have the seller carry a $15,000.00 second (OWNER MORTGAGE). Look at the first comparable below.

	First Comparable	Second Comparable
BALANCE DUE (first mortgage)	$35,000.00	$35,000.00
DOWN PAYMENT	$10,000.00	$10,000.00
OWNER MORTGAGE	$15,000.00	$17,000.00
TOTAL AMOUNT OF OFFER	$60,000.00	$62,000.00

The interest rate is negotiable with the seller, and you will need an amortization book to determine your monthly payments on the second (owner) mortgage. The $15,000.00 could be paid to the seller at 12% for 25 years. The monthly payment would then be $157.99 as indicated by the #1 offer of section 3.

	1st. Offer	2nd. Offer	3rd. Offer
BANK MORTGAGE	$ 394.91	$ 394.91	$
OWNER MORTGAGE	$ 157.99	$ 131.21	$
TAXES	$ 175.00	$ 175.00	$
INSURANCE	$ 24.00	$ 24.00	$
WATER	$ 45.00	$ 45.00	$
GAS	$	$	$
ELECTRIC	$	$	$
MAINTENANCE	$ 33.75	$ 33.75	$
TOTAL COST	$ 830.65	$ 803.87	$

On the other hand, if the seller wants his total equity of $25,000.00 in cash, we know this offer probably will not be accepted. If the seller is only concerned with a higher selling price, and doesn't care about interest rate, we could increase the offer to $62,000.00 in an attempt to convince him to hold the second mortgage. He would get what he wants, so now he would take our $10,000.00 down payment and carry a second mortgage of $17,000.00. Let's set the interest rate at 8% for 25 years and see what happens. The monthly payment is now in our favor at $131.21 per month. Notice that payments on $17,000.00 over the same period of time (25 years), with just a 4% reduction in the interest rate is $26.78 less than the payment on $15,000.00. Do not underestimate the impact of interest rates. Try to use this section of the form to structure all your real estate deals.

Just a suggestion here, when you make your inspection of the property, write a list of all negatives and/or repairs needed, but do not discuss them with the seller at this point. When the negotiations start, the seller most likely will want to raise your offering price for some things that he sees as assets or positive points about the property. When he brings up the "newly painted deck", you might mention, yes "but the garage door needs repair" and get back to the negotiations. In other words if he mention an asset, you mention a liability, if he doesn't go there, then your negotiation should proceed well. If you don't need to mention the negatives, then don't. If you had discussed these negatives when you first saw them, the seller will feel that those issues were already addressed, and still want the extra compensation for the positives that he brings up.

There are a lot of great books out there dealing with making offers! I heard of a guy talking about how he always offered a low-ball figure to the seller, and unsurprisingly when it was rejected, he had 3 or 4 better offers in his coat pocket. He'd pull out the next offer and say "what about this one". He said most times at some point, he had an offer that the seller would consider. But he also pondered something else that was very interesting. It seemed to make him a bit disturbed when the seller accepted the first offer. Why? He was wondering how low of an offer would the seller have accepted!

Cost Information Section.

SECTION 4. The COST section was devised to list and break down each expense by month. As mentioned earlier, if you do not have an approximate amount to put on these lines, use some rule of thumb (a percentage of income, a certain amount per apartment, etc.) The water and maintenance cost can be figured as a rule of thumb. I used $15.00 per apartment per month for water which amounts to $45.00 for three apartments, and 3% of income for maintenance (even the most well-kept homes need repairs every now and then). The total income is $1,125.00 per month so the 3% maintenance is $33.75 per month or $405.00 a year. If these costs are higher or lower in your area, adjust them accordingly. The reason for this is that such items as repairs and water bills are real dollar expenses that will vary each month. Despite the fact that we sometimes do not know the exact amounts, we must project them because we will surely have to pay for these expenditures at some point in time.

You might say $405.00 is a low amount for repairs a year, but considering some years nothing goes wrong, but other years believe me a whole lot could go wrong. If you put that 3% maintenance fee in the bank for 20 years, you would have over $8,000.00 saved. If you think you need more, start depositing away 5% for repairs. Just, be prepared for repair cost.

The taxes are $2,100.00 per year or $175.00 per month. Insurance payments for the year amounts to $288.00 a year, which equals $24.00 per month.

The lines for gas and electric bills are only used if the owner supplies the utilities for the tenant. If this three family house had only one electric meter, one gas meter, and one furnace, the utilities would obviously have to be paid by the owner, as there is no way to break down the consumption of each separate apartment.

I personally will not pay the utilities as mentioned earlier! If there is only one furnace, I always put in one for each apartment, split the electric, and have the gas and electric company install separate meters for each apartment. This way the tenant can be responsible for his or her own consumption. Also if the tenant leaves without paying, you lose only your rental income, but you would not incur the tenant's utility bills to boot. To make things simple in our example, we have three apartments, three gas meters, and three electric meters, and the tenant's pay their own.

Profit Information Section.

Section 5. (Profit Information) /

	1ˢᵀ Offer	2ⁿᵈ Offer	3ʳᵈ Offer
INCOME	$ 1,125.00	$ 1,125.00	$
EXPENSES	$ 830.00	$ 803.87	$
CASH FLOW	$ 294.35	$ 321.13	$

Section 5, is PROFIT, and it is vital that you have one. For our sample case, we will be using the second offer. We know what the monthly expenses are, or at least have estimated them to be $803.87, and we know that the income is $1,125.00. We will subtract monthly expenses from monthly income to get $321.13, which is a close "ball park" figure of what we can expect our cash flow to be. Boy! You talk about bottom line' well, this is it. THIS IS IT!!! If you multiply this figure by 12, you will get $3,853.00, your profit for the year.

Cash On Cash Return.

Now, if you wish, you can figure your "Cash return on investment" to determine how quickly you are going to re-coupe your down payment. You know that there are other benefits such as Appreciation, Equity Build-up, and Depreciation, but let's concentrate on the dollar for dollar return right now.

Let's refer to our example where we offered $10,000.00 as a down payment, and calculated the cash flow for the year to be $3,853.56. We divide one year's profit ($3,853.56) by the down payment ($10,000.00) to get a 38.5 per cent return on this investment the first year.

It will take just about two and a half years to get your $10,000.00 out of pocket DOWNPAYMENT back. Think about what this really amounts to, ask a Banker If you can get a double your money investment at his establishment in a five years period of time, if you want to hear some loud laughter. Not a bad investment, you say, but if you had worked for a "nothing down" deal, forget about trying to figure cash on cash return; everything is gravy!

If you had the confidence to make such a real estate purchase, you could have this cash flow for as long as you decide to hold the property. Just think, if you had ten or twenty of these you could be your own boss, and make profits at whatever level that you were comfortable with. In fact, when inflation drives prices up, rents go up as well, and that means more cash flow for you on each property that you own. By the way, if you keep this property pass the agreed 25 years, what happens to those mortgage payments you were sending to the sellers? They are deposited to your very own "Hip National Bank", you get to keep those payments, that's what! You now own it free and clear for as long as you desire.

NOTE$

_____

_____

_____

_____

_____

_____

_____

_____

_____

_____

_____

_____

_____

_____

_____

_____

_____

_____

_____

_____

_____

CHAPTER 5

6
THE TENANT AND YOUR APARTMENT

COLLECTION STRATEGIES FOR THE REAL ESTATE OWNER,
LANDLORD, AND PROPERTY MANAGER.

Screening The Prospective Tenant.

It all begins when you get a call from a person wanting information about your "Apartment for Rent". When you answer the phone, smile (even though the person can't see you), be pleasant and polite. After your introduction, begin screening the caller to save valuable time. First, get their name, current address, age, marital status and other pertinent information. Ask the reason they are moving from their last apartment. Ask if they have notified their present landlord of their intention to move. If the caller starts telling you how terrible the current landlord is, be cautious, you may be a lease signing away from being the current landlord.

If you have more than one apartment available, find out which one the caller is inquiring about. Mention the amount of the rent and advise that there is a Security Deposit required. At this point, wait for a reaction from the caller. You must know that this information is vital, so if there is no response, ask the caller if this amount fits their budget. Do not leave this point until you get an answer, because you could go through the entire process to find that the caller either has no money, or not enough money to rent your apartment.

Some young prospects do not fully understand responsibility. One told me that they had no money, but was going to borrow the first month's rent from a friend. They lived with a cousin, and they had no car, but had filled out a couple of job application questionnaires. At the end of the phone interview, they asked when they could pick up the keys. I asked if they were listening to the interview we just had and if they heard the answers that they gave to me, before I rejected the request for tenancy.

You need to ask questions that will alert you as to how the caller matches up with your vacancy. You will also want to find out how soon the person needs the Apartment. They may be inquiring to take possession of the apartment two or three months from now, when in fact you may be looking to rent the apartment on the first day of next month.

Next ask the caller about their family size, and whether or not they have a pet. These question will reveal if the caller has children or pets (of course it's your decision, but I advise you not to accept pets, as some do a lot of damage, smell, and often carry fleas and ticks if not properly cared for).

If it looks as though the caller qualifies for the apartment, find out if the apartment qualifies for the caller. Ask if they have any special requirements. If they start asking about "nearby Schools", "public transportation, "big back yard, "air conditioning", or any other assets that are not available in your apartment, discuss these issues with them right now, before you waste time going to the property. Some of these things could be deal breakers.

Decide If "TENANT" And "APARTMENT" Match.

If at any point in the conversation, you realize that the person does not qualify for your apartment or the apartment is not what the person is looking for, end the call in a courteous manner. If on the other hand, everything checks out, make an appointment to show the apartment. If the caller is married, schedule the appointment at a time when both the husband and wife can meet with you.

When you meet the prospective tenants, try to make a good first impression. Be on time and greet them with a smile and a firm handshake. Make sure that the apartment is in good shape, clean, and ready to be shown. Act professionally, speak clearly, and be aware of your appearance.

Have the prospective tenant fill out a Rental Application (see page 104), and check to make sure it is completed properly. The information that you obtain may become vital in later months. After your initial discussion and showing, you may want to call some of the references, check his job information, contact the current landlord, or even stop by to see how they keep up their current apartment.

After talking with and sizing up the prospective tenant and they are sure they want the apartment, you must decide if this prospective tenant is right for your apartment. If they are acceptable, at some point you will have them sign the Rental Agreement (see page 113) and <u>collect the rent and security deposit</u>. Please do not start out behind the 8-ball, if the tenant does not have the rent and/or the security deposit. You should have asked this question, before you made the appointment to meet them. Question to prospective tenant on the phone; - will you have all of the rent and all of the security deposit when we meet? -The total is ($) sum! -Will you have that exact amount? You do not want to get to the meeting place to find that the tenant mis-calculated.

Please note on the Rental Agreement where you see;

> This agreement shall begin _____ and end on _____.
> Tenant may renew for additional term, **MONTH TO MONTH** thereafter.

The <u>agreement</u> term is one month, it's the beginning and the ending dates of the first month.

- - for example; "begin ___ Jan. 1<u>st</u>, 2016 ___ and end on ___ Jan. 30, 2016 ___.

<u>MONTH TO MONTH</u> refers to the ongoing months to follow (renewing automatically).

You will want to walk-through the property at this time with the tenant (again if necessary) and complete the "Property Condition Report" (see page 111) at this time. Have the tenant sign, then you sign -before you give them the keys.

Do Not Discriminate.

If you feel the individual is unsuitable for some reason, tell them now. Be careful here, whatever your reason, stay within the law. Acceptable reasons for refusing tenancy are a poor credit rating, a criminal record, a history of eviction, lies on the application, failure to keep last apartment neat and clean, insufficient income, or does not have the money to cover all of the rent and all of the security deposit at this present time.

You cannot reject a prospective tenant on the basis of sex, marital status, race, color, ethnic background, or religion. Discrimination is a crime.

The Problem Tenant.

Problem tenants move around, so if you don't have them, chances are you will get one sooner or later. First and always, remember that tenants are people too! With that in mind, let's turn our attention, and talk about bad tenants for a moment. All the screening in the world still will not weed out all of the bad ones, because some will get through.

There are tenants that view the landlord as their personal slave, they want to give orders, they want the landlord to jump when they say jump. Some have that bad attitude in general, seem like their lot in life is to torture the landlord. They may start out so humble in the beginning, until they take the keys from your hand. It could be good and bad right now, but it can get truly ugly in the months to come. You can see the change sometime, look right into their eyes when you put the keys into their hands, see that look, it's like they're thinking "I got you now, you're mine".

There are a small amount of professional tenants out there who will pay the first month's rent and a security deposit to get their foot in the door, with the thought of living rent-free for the next six to eight months. The key is tenant selection, so screen well, and knowing the "System". This could make your land lording experience so much better.

There are some tenants who have good intentions, but who cannot afford the apartment they are applying for. Some tenants, after they're already in the property will find a problem, or create one, just to withhold your rent. When this happens, you had better know the "System".

I visited one tenant in one of my property after I rented to her and found that the apartment was filled with just a few trashy items. I asked what happened to all that nice furniture she had in her last apartment where I visited her, and then she told me that it was her parent's apartment.

Don't misunderstand, most renters pay on time and without problems, but this section is dedicated to that small percentage that do not. If you are involved in renting property, chances are good that you will get a problem tenant, and you will need to know how to deal with the situation. Check out the "System" in chapter 9.

Tenant Responsibilities.

Responsibilities of the tenant vary from state to state, and from one area of the country to another. There are, however, some generally accepted responsibilities for the tenant. Tenants are required to treat the property in a responsible manner, pay the rent on time, keep their own apartment sanitary, and free from insects, and rodents (If the whole building is infested, it could be the landlord's responsibility to exterminate). The tenant must notify the landlord of any needed repairs or unsafe conditions, and allow no additional people to become permanent residents. However, they have the right to have guests visit them for reasonable periods. A tenant must respect the rights of other tenants and avoid damaging the property. If they or their guests cause any damage, the tenant is responsible for repairing it.

If the tenant does not honor their responsibilities, you may evict them. Tenants also have an obligation to give you proper notice if they intend to leave. If they are renting with a lease, they must give whatever length of notice that is indicated in the lease. Otherwise, they must give you notice at least 30 days before the next rent is due, if your month to month rental agreement specifies this. Make sure that your lease or rental agreement covers these obligations.

Leasing: "ADVANTAGE OR DISADVANTAGE".

You should know when to lease and when to rent on a month-to-month bases. There are both advantages and disadvantages to you in having a lease, and you must make your decision based on your individual circumstances. A lease is a legal contract between landlord and tenant, which can be either verbal or written. A verbal lease is considered just as binding as a written one, so long as it is for no longer than one year's duration. However, you should keep in mind that with a verbal contract, it is often difficult for both parties to remember exactly what was agreed on, and what was said at a later time.

A lease generally assures you that your property will be occupied for a specific length of time, but prevents you from evicting and raising the rent during that period unless you have included an escalation clause to cover increases resulting from such things as property tax, insurance, water, etc. Your lease should define these charges as "additional rent". If you want to ask a tenant to leave, or change some other aspect of the rental agreement, you must usually wait until the lease expires.

A lease does offer the advantage of spelling out the specific rights and responsibilities of each party. This sort of clear, written account will go far toward avoiding possible future conflicts. Consult your attorney if you have any question about the validity of a clause you wish to include in a lease.

Without a written or verbal lease, the rental agreement is assumed to operate on a month-to-month basis. Unless either party gives notice 30 days before the rent payment is due, the tenancy is automatically renewed for the following month. A tenant who is in possession of the apartment on the day the rent is due owes the full amount of rent for that month. If you evict, the judge may pro-rate the rent for the actual total number of days that the tenant has possession.

Lease Requirements.

If you decide to require a written lease, it must be in the "Plain English" format. Leases are available through legal printers and at some stationery stores. These leases can be amended if both you and your tenant agree to the modifications. Both parties need only initial the changes in the margin of the lease. You will see a written lease on page 105.

Your lease should state clearly and precisely, any penalty which will be imposed upon a tenant who wishes to move out before the lease expires. If no penalty is specified, the tenant is liable for the rent of the entire lease term. To collect this rent, however, you may have to go to court and prove that you made a good-faith effort to re-rent the apartment after the tenant moved out.

One solution which landlords often find workable, is to allow the tenant who wants to get out of a lease to assign or sublet the apartment; that is, to find a new tenant to live there. In fact, if the property you own has four or more living units, you might be required to offer the tenant this option. You can, however, insist on your approval of any new tenant moving in.

Collect The Late Charges.

Always collect your late charges if provided for in your lease or rental agreement. Late charges have a two-fold purpose; first to improve collections by discouraging the tenant from paying late and second, for recoupment of some of the collection cost. Late charges should only be waived when the tenant has an emergency beyond his or her control. Don't get into the habit of accepting just any excuse the tenant gives. By so-doing, you may find yourself in the position of automatically waiving the late charges. This is counter-productive, defeating the purpose behind the tenant-landlord arrangement.

Get A Security Deposit.

A security deposit from your tenants will help assure you against property damage or the loss of rent from the tenant leaving without prior notice. Such a deposit, usually equal in amount to one month's rent, and is held by you for the duration of the tenancy.

You do not have to allow the tenant to use the security deposit to cover the last month's rent, but you do have to return it within a reasonable time after the tenant move out, providing that the tenants have not damaged the apartment, and they have given you proper notice of their intention to leave. This means that the tenant must give you whatever length of notice is specified in the lease or, if there is no lease, they must tell you 30 days before the rent is due that they intend to move.

In order to avoid disputes over damages, I recommend that the landlord and the tenants inspect the apartment together, both when the tenants move in and again when they move out. The Property Condition Report (check-list) can be seen on page 111.

The Security Deposit Is The Tenant's Money.

You may not withhold money from the security deposit for anything that constitutes normal wear and tear, only for actual damages to the property that are the obligation of the tenant. Any money you withhold from your tenants security deposits should be documented by receipts for all materials and contractors services necessary to repair the damage. Copies of these receipts should be made available to the tenants if they wish to see them. Such documentation will also help you defend the deductions should the tenant decide to challenge them in Small Claims Court.

You must keep your tenants security deposits separate from your own money. If you rent six or more apartments in the same building or complex, you may be required to keep the security deposit in an interest-bearing account, and pay the interest to the tenant.

The tenant is entitled to know where their money is being kept, and how much interest it is earning. When you return the interest to the tenant, you may be entitled to one percentage point for administering the account. For instance, if the bank pays 5 percent interest, you must pay the tenant at least 4 percent.

When Can You Enter A Tenant's Apartment.

You should know under what circumstances you can enter a tenant's apartment. Many leases specify that a landlord may enter the apartment at any time, to make repairs or to show the unit to a prospective new tenant. However, even with such a clause, you should use restraint in exercising this right. General practice is to notify the tenant at least 24 hours in advance of your intent to enter. You should also arrange to make the visit at a reasonable hour.

Of course, in an emergency you may enter the apartment immediately, without notice. If a tenant changes the locks to the apartment, you may demand a new key so that you will have access in an emergency.

The tenant has the right to "quiet enjoyment" of their apartment, free from interference, as long as they uphold their end of the rental agreement. Your repeated and unnecessary entries, without good reason, could lead to legal action against you.

Don't Mix Business With Pleasure.

Now, a gigantic warning to you about some tenants (Okay, gentleman), never, ever, under any circumstances, let yourself become sexually involved, or have any type of affair with a tenant. For the minute you do, you're on a slippery slope to disaster. I could mention some stories that I've heard about landlords and tenants, but the rating of this book would have to be changed to XXX, so you'll just have to take my word on this one.

You'll probably meet a lot of willing, would be easy, opportunistic renters out there, but you would do well to heed my warning, and put this high on your list of "do not's". If you give in to temptation, I suggest you pray very hard, because you have a good chance of providing a rent-free apartment for that tenant for as long as they want it, with your investment career in jeopardy, and your own personal reputation and dignity hanging in the balance.

Armed with these facts, you would be wise to stay away from those quick and inviting emotional temptations. Me personally, I have an even better motive, my wife don't allow me to court.

NOTE$

_____

_____

_____

_____

_____

_____

_____

_____

_____

_____

_____

_____

_____

_____

_____

_____

_____

_____

_____

CHAPTER 6

7

DIALING FOR DOLLARS

COLLECTION STRATEGIES FOR THE REAL ESTATE OWNER, LANDLORD, AND PROPERTY MANAGER.

Successful Collection Through Telephone Calls.

Every collection call for rent should be business-like, firm and fair with the intention of getting a specific amount, date, and time the tenant will pay. You must conduct a prompt and persuasive collection call. You should educate the tenant and help with complaints, if necessary. Keep good follow-up records, or the tenant will not take your collection efforts seriously. Be persistent and stress the importance of paying the rents on time.

When you get the tenant on the line (make sure you're talking to the right person), be pleasant and tell him who you are. Tell him that you are calling about the past due rent payment, and then pause. This gives the tenant an opportunity to explain his situation. Usually he will tell you the reason he didn't pay, and give you an indication of when he will pay.

Listen to his explanation, you are on the phone, and you can't get the payment in your hand anyway. Maybe you could offer some helpful advice after you have reviewed the facts. You can discuss any complaints as the conversation progresses. Often, slow payments are due to some tenant dissatisfaction.

Make realistic arrangements; be sure that they are reasonable and definite. You should repeat the arrangements to the tenant, and make him aware that you are putting the arrangements into writing. Be specific, and repeat the payment amount, the date, and the time that the rent will be paid.

You are also interested in the tenant paying on time every month, so in closing the call, ask whether there will be a problem with the rent in the upcoming month, or if you can expect the rent on time.

Chronic Delinquents.

There is a big distinction between a long term tenant who always paid on time being late, as opposed to the chronic delinquent. You can believe that there must be a real problem with the long term good tenant, this is not his norm, so don't get too forward with him, and stir easy as you communicate with him. You can be more understanding and lenient with this person than with a person who pays late all the time.

The Chronic delinquent tenant is best handled in person, but if you must talk to him by phone, educate him regarding the necessity of timely payments. This tenant requires firmer handling, so don't let him think you can be put off.

Don't be brushed off by some fast and vague promise to pay. Only specific amount, for specific dates and specific times are acceptable.

If you feel the tenant won't pay when he says he will, don't agree to the promise he makes. If your efforts have no effect and the delinquency continues or the tenant becomes troublesome, it may be best to give him a notice to vacate the premises (we'll go into details in a later chapter).

Educate The Tenant.

What's involved in educating the tenant? Let the tenant know that first, foremost, and always – THE RENT MUST BE PAID IN FULL AND ON TIME. Nearly everything else can be worked out in a landlord/tenant relationship. Payment of rent is non-negotiable.

Let the tenant know that if there are any problems in the apartment, they must be reported to you when they occur, and not wait until the rent is due. Some tenants will fine (or create) a problem with the apartment, in an attempt to withhold the rent.

You should convey your regrets for any dissatisfaction the tenant might have for whatever reason, but let the tenant know that the rental agreement terms must be met. Insist that the rent be paid on time. Make a note of any complaints, and advise the tenant when you can possibly correct the problems.

Advise the tenant that their car payment, credit card bill, or any other monthly payment is not an acceptable excuse for not paying the rent on time. For every tenant that you successfully educate to pay when due, you will reclaim more of your time for doing other things.

Telephone Calls But Tenant Never Home.

Should you find it necessary to attempt to contact the tenant by phone for any reason (but especially in the case of delinquent rent), do not embarrass the tenant by discussing the matter with a third party. If you call and are informed that the tenant is not in, try to get as much information as you can. Typical questions might include; "when are you expecting him/her home?" and "Is there another number at which they can be reached?" You must use tact if you have to call a tenant at work.

It is a good idea to find out the name of the person with whom you are speaking and ask that person to have the tenant return your call. Being precise, to the point, and non-threatening may help to insure that the person will have the tenant return your call.

If you cannot reach the tenant in the morning, try at noon, and again at different times of the afternoon and night.

If you are speaking with a child on the phone, you should bear in mind that children are unreliable message-takers and deliverers, and it may be necessary for you to follow-up at a later time. You should keep a record of the dates and times of your phone calls to the tenant's apartment, along with a notation of who you spoke with, and the message you left.

Making A Personal Contact At The Property.

If you find that the tenant does not return your calls and is often not in when you call, it may be avoidance on his or her part. In this case, a personal visit maybe needed. If you get to the door and they are truly trying to avoid contact with you, it's time to put the system to use.

Once as I approached the home, I saw the curtain move and one of the kids came to the door and announced "my mother said to tell you that she's not home". Well, being an experienced collector, I instructed the kid to go back into the house and ask the mother "what time would she expect to be home", and the door closed abruptly. I had my answer and the "system" (see Chapter 9) was in full blown mode.

Broken Promises To Pay The Rent.

You should be much firmer with a tenant who has broken a promise to you. Find out why he failed to contact you when he found that he couldn't keep his promise.

Impose a sense of urgency, asks the tenant to bring the rent to you immediately. Don't take another promise unless you are convinced that the tenant will keep his promise.

Tenant Loses His Job.

If you reach a tenant who tells you that he has just lost his job, you should be prepared to ask a series of questions. You will need to know if he's going to stay, or if he will have to move because of this misfortune.

Pertinent questions may include requesting such information as to whether or not the separation from his job is temporary or permanent, and when the employment was terminated; whether the tenant has any other source of income, severance pay or back pay entitlement that would assist in paying the rent; whether or not unemployment insurance eligibility has been explored and the status of it; the possibility of borrowing some funds from family, friends or other sources; whether or not the spouse, if there is one, could handle the rent until such time as the tenant is again gainfully employed.

Asking questions to obtain the above information may help you to assist the tenant with his problem, as there may be some solutions he has not thought of. If nothing more, it will at least let you know where both of you stand in the situation. Should you keep getting negative responses to the question you pose, it may be necessary to simply ask the tenant point blank, "will you still be able to afford the apartment".

Tenant Files Bankruptcy.

If a tenant files Bankruptcy, it should not affect your rental situation at all, check with your attorney. The only affect it might have is if the tenant owes you money at the time of filing, and the tenant names you as an unsecured creditor on the petition of Bankruptcy.

Contact your attorney immediately if this happens, because it may preclude you from collecting any money as for as past due rents are concerned. It may also be necessary to make application in the Bankruptcy Court to lift the "stay". In some cases this can be done before the first meeting of the creditors.

Bankruptcy would not normally prevent an owner from collecting rents or evicting the tenant. The owner should, however, update his records and determine where the tenant can be reached day and night. Verify all information on the rental application and make an appointment to discuss the situation with the tenant in person, if necessary.

When the owner meets with the tenant, nothing should be said to alienate the tenant. The owner should determine the tenant's intentions at this point. Then, keep complete and accurate records of your conversation with the tenant.

Tenant Dies.

If one of your tenants dies, it would be in your best interest to have a completed and up-to-date rental application with the nearest relative indicated so that you may contact the appropriate person to remove the tenant's possessions. If the relative has moved and you are unsuccessful in locating him/her, check the application for a friend who might be able to assist you in locating a relative of the deceased.

If none of the above is applicable, contact the executor of the deceased's estate and request in writing that the tenant's belongings be removed from the premises.

If none of this works, you can remove and store the property yourself. You should write a certified letter to whomever is listed on the rental application; explain that the property will be stored by you for thirty days. If you still have not heard anything by the end of that period, call the property clerk, the town clerk, or the Sheriff's Department for instruction for disposal. Again, check with your attorney in case there is a different process where you are located.

Collection Record.

In the next chapter we will be discussing collections by personal contact, so I have devised a form that I call the "Collection Record/ Rent Schedule". It is used to post rent payments and record information as I work on a tenant's account. I make out one form for each tenant. These forms are kept in a control book. A sample of the form can be seen on page 112.

The current year goes at the top, then the address, tenant's name, employer, phone number, rent amount, date due, amount of security deposit, and the dates tenant moved in and out. This is most of the information that you would normally need when you go out in the field to collect. This section is found on the left hand side of the form and is self-explanatory.

On the right side of the form, there are 12 columns to record the dates and amounts of rents collected or received for one full year.

The comment section at the bottom of the form is very important, you can make notes of anything from a date to inspect the property, to recording the bank name and account number of a check the tenant gives you, to jotting down the plate number of a car that is in the driveway (the back of the form can be used when you run out of room on the front). All this information may be helpful in the future.

Make sure you take this form with you when you go out to collect, and update it at every opportunity. For instance, a tenant asks you to call her at a friend's house later, and she gives you the friends name and number. Don't just throw the information away after you have used it; put it on the form because it may be useful in the future. It could save you a lot of time and trouble.

Later, if that tenant's home phone is disconnected, or changed, or unlisted, you might be able to get the new number from that friend, or at least leave a message for the tenant to return your call. Recognize the importance of posting your follow-up information on this form, because you will not remember everything. Write it down in a place where you can find it.

NOTE$

_____

_____

_____

_____

_____

_____

_____

_____

_____

_____

_____

_____

_____

_____

_____

_____

_____

_____

_____

_____

_____

CHAPTER 7

8

THE PHILOSOPHY OF COLLECTING

COLLECTION STRATEGIES FOR THE REAL ESTATE OWNER,
LANDLORD, AND PROPERTY MANAGER.

Collection Qualifications And Professional Experience.

I think credibility is important here, so I will tell you a little about myself, my qualifications and my professional experiences. I feel that a real estate career was just made for me, because it fits right into my area of expertise on all accounts. On a daily basis I manage people, keep records, and collect rents. Before I go any farther, you need to know where I received my training to understand my credibility, and be confident that I know what I am talking about.

I was raised in Dothan, Al and I have many fond memories of this place. I graduated from Carver High School. This is where I learned about morals, truth telling, about believing in God, and employing a strong work ethic. The Parents, Teachers, Pastors, and all the Neighbors had an obligation to make sure kids and young adults were doing the right things.

I was trained as an Administrative Specialist in the United States Air Force. I served four years, and my primary Duty Station was Charleston Air Force Base South Carolina where I obtained the rank of Sargent and was Honorably Discharged in 1970.

I received a college Associate Degree funded with my Veterans Benefits from LaSalle Extension University. I majored in Business Management and maintained a B plus average.

For over fifteen years I worked at G.M.A.C (General Motors Acceptance Corporation), the fully-owned financial arm of General Motors. It is important to note that the collectors trained by General Motors are among the best in the entire world.

The fact that some car owners do not make their payments in a timely manner is not surprising. I was a Credit Representative, and collector, with the responsibility of approximately 5,000 such accounts. I was well-trained, took my work seriously, and achieved some impressive results. This experience was very helpful to me as I became involved in the collection of rents.

Similarities And Differences Between Real Estate And Auto's.

When I began buying houses, I discovered that there were some similarities and differences between real estate rents and automobile payments. The first thing that I noticed similarly, was that some tenants pay on time in an orderly manner and some do not. I found that with certain types of people, you have to be the first one at the door to get the money. When I went to collect car payments, the tenants said "I had to pay the rent" (#1 excuse).

For that very reason, I stopped asking why tenants didn't have the money. They have become experienced in what to say to people to whom they owe money. You are not the only one collecting from these people. Believe me; they have more answers than you have questions, and they are armed with many, many reasons. When you call or go out to collect, the question is always when! Not what or why. So, never ask why. Some tenants can articulate such a sad condition or excuse that you'll feel so much sorrow for them that you'll be crying in your beer. Some narratives are so believable, that you'll be ready to donate to the cause they have presented, and you might even consider making them a loan. Remember, don't say "what happened", they are just waiting for you to ask that question; it's like "ah ha, I got you". So, ask "when will you pay?" because that's what you really want to know, isn't it?

Some people never pay on time, even if they have the money. We use to call them "Chronical Delinquents" (among other things) when I worked at GMAC. You have to recognize a "Milk Run", the customer who knows they're supposed to put the rent in the mail each month, but you have to physically be at the door with your hand out to get it. If you go to collect, and no one is home, put a notice under the door to let the tenant know you have been there and have not forgotten him.

Now, let's take a brief look at some of the differences between collection services for rents and automobiles. One of the major differences is that cars move but houses do not. Often, before you can collect on an automobile account, it is necessary to locate the auto in question. If the owner moves without informing you, you are faced with locating the individual and the car, or you risk losing an auto worth a possible $18,000.00 (or more), depending on the year, make, and model of the car. The difference here is that in real estate, the house is stationary and if the tenant is one who has no intention of paying the rent or is unable to do so, you would be better off if he did move. I've never had a tenant drive off in one of my properties.

If the purchaser pays off the car, it becomes his property. On the other hand, if the tenant pays off your house, it remains your possession. I hope you're taking notes.

You Have To Collect.

There is another important difference between real estate and the auto industry I would like to mention here. Should they locate the car (and most times they do), they can repossess it and get some, or all of the money back by sale at public auction. With a tenant, even though he's right there, if you let him get behind in the rent, especially if he's over extended, chances are you will never see a dime of the money after he moves. Sure, you could go to court, pay the cost and take time, maybe pay an attorney to get a judgement, but all you get is another piece of paper affirming that the tenant owes you money.

That's what a judgement is; it's still up to you to collect that rent the tenant owes you. Sometimes you get the money by acquiring a judgement, but it did not happen often enough for me. The funny thing about that is, you already had a piece of paper saying the tenant owed you money before you paid that court cost, it's call a rental agreement or a lease. Very hard to get your money after the tenant vacates, just judging for what you could do with it, sometimes the judgement is not worth the paper it's written on, it's related to what you can do with toilet tissue.

Since you know you have to collect it, do it while the tenant is still in your property, or evict him before he owes you more that he can pay. When he leaves, there is no collateral implied on your Rental Agreement or Lease Contract. Unpaid rents are unsecured debts, and you have two chances of collecting them after the tenant has moved out, slim and none (and slim just left town).

Personally, I have never known an owner who has recouped all of his delinquent rents from a tenant, after the tenant had already moved out. I've seen owners pay out extra money to get a judgement, but it all boils down to the same thing: YOU HAVE TO COLLECT THE RENT. You could hire a Sheriff or Marshal at another extra expense to try to collect a judgement (this is unrecoverable overhead), but even they can't get blood from a turnip. They can't do a thing if the person owns nothing of value, has no money in the bank, is not working, or is self-employed. If you had wanted to pay someone, you could have hired an independent property management company to collect the rents for you while the tenant was still in the property in the first place. This is also a gamble, however, unless it's an exceptional management company. I have to disclose that after many years, and stacks of judgements, I did receive a very small amount from a collection agency. It could never be worth it, less than 1% of what was owed, and the collection agency took half of that. Moral of this story is, dedicate the majority of your collection efforts to the period where it counts the most, while the tenant is still in your apartment.

Philosophy Of Collecting.

The dictionary describes the meaning of collect as; "to gather payments" and "a soliciting of money", but there's another element involved, and that is, the philosophy of collecting. This element concerns the nature of human values and beliefs. Provided you have given the tenant true value, meaning a decent place to live, then the sincere tenant must feel obligated to compensate you for that value, and also know that there is a penalty for non-performance.

You have to believe in yourself, you must believe that you have the just authority to collect, and you must make the tenant believe it. If tenants think you are a pushover, then they are going to push you over.

Otherwise stated, the tenant has to pay the rent or he must move, and he understands the arrangement absolutely without a doubt. This feeling is inescapable if you have a good lease or rental agreement, and you have a good system to enforce it.

Most Common Reasons Tenants Do Not Pay.

Even the most experienced collector will tell you that sometimes things go wrong and rents cannot be collected for one reason or another. We have already been introduced to some of them earlier in this chapter under the section entitled "Similarities And Differences Between Real Estate And Auto's". There are other reasons, however, for which things go wrong, and one of the most important of these is that tenants fail to budget. They do not prioritize (that is, pay the most important bills first). That nets out to "first come, first served" most times for the collector. Often there are other legitimate reasons such as unforeseen expenses and the tenant has overestimated his capacity to pay.

There are times when a tenant feels it's within his right to withhold rent payments deliberately. This may result from the presence of "unhealthy" or "unsafe" conditions present at the premises. In some rare instances, you may encounter an individual who simply does not intend to pay, no matter what goods or services they have received. These are reasons for delinquency that you, as a collector will have to analyze and respond to quickly. After reading chapter 9, you will know how to correctly handle these common situations.

Tenants will give you many reasons for late payments, and most will fall into one or more of the above categories. For instance, a tenant says "My father unexpectedly died and I had to help pay for the burial". Provided he's telling you the truth, this is "unforeseen expenses". If the tenant says "his car payment was due", this means either he is not able to afford both the car payment and the rent, "has over-estimated his capacity to pay", or he "didn't budget" and the car collector and other creditors got there first. By the way, the #1 excuse, now that I'm collecting rent is, you guessed it "I had to pay the car payment".

It will be advantageous at this point to find out the real problem here, so you can proceed to rectify the situation. If the tenant is never home, or says "I didn't get my check", or "the rent check is in the mail" watch out. He could be the one who does not intend to pay, or he could be simply utilizing a delay ploy to get more time. He could be just putting you off. We use to refer to it as "employing the stall".

NOTE$

CHAPTER 8

9

COLLECTING RENT "THE SYSTEM"

COLLECTION STRATEGIES FOR THE REAL ESTATE OWNER, LANDLORD, AND PROPERTY MANAGER.

Here's The "SYSTEM".

Now we get down to business, down to the nitty gritty. This is where the rubber meets the road (a little saying that I picked up working in the Auto Industry). I will share with you a system that I created out of necessity when I began investing in real estate in the state of New York (your laws could be different). At the time, I had been trained in and was working a full-time job (including overtime and weekends as required) as a collector. This "System" was devised for the purpose of helping to timely manage proven and consistent problem tenants.

My system is graduated, step by step, utilizing the least expensive and most effective methods available to me at the time. The effort increases in firmness and receives more personal attention as the past due rent collection procedure progresses through the various steps.

Satisfactory collection performance is based on a balanced

collection effort, with each step being essential to the success of the overall effort. I strongly suggest that you control your profits and learn to use these next few steps.

–SIGNED AGREEMENT–.

STEP 1. (day 1) Have a well written Rental Agreement or Lease signed by the tenant. In order to demand certain things from a tenant (that the rent be paid on time, for instance) you must have him sign a contract that lists the conditions (ground rules if you will), that must be followed (for our example, the rent is due on the 1st of each month). I have provided a Lease on page 105 and a Rental Agreement on page 113.

Read each of them carefully and make sure you have a thorough understanding of each. Depending on the law where you live, it may be necessary to make some changes (consult your attorney). Every statement and condition on these forms is for your protection, and you should know what they mean. The tenant may even ask you to explain certain parts of these forms. These strong clauses give you the "hammer" legally. Whether you enforce them or not, is up to you.

–RENT AND SECURITY DEPOSIT–.

STEP 2 (day 1) Get a month's rent and a Security Deposit before the tenant moves in. You will see why this is so important later on. Even if the tenant pays the rent on time and does no damage, the security deposit gives that extra incentive to leave the apartment in a clean and orderly condition, also to move out and return the keys to you on or before the rent is due for the next month. In addition, tenants always seem to be much nicer, and have a pleasanter attitude when you have a Security Deposit that may be returned to them.

Always remember that the Security Deposit belongs to the tenant and should not be used for your personal expenses. Morality and integrity must prevail here, for the money does not belong to you. If a tenant moves out when it's time, leaving the apartment in reasonable good and clean condition, return the Security Deposit. Until that time, it should be placed in escrow, or you may set up a separate savings account for that purpose, as I do.

–CONTACT TENANT IN PERSON–.

STEP 3 (day 1 thru 5) Make a personal contact by the 5th of the month if the rent has not been received (you can call anytime in between). You may want to phone the tenant, but all you can get if you talk to the tenant by phone is an explanation of why the rent wasn't paid, or some promise to mail it, but we are looking for the rent, *now*. Let's say the tenant rent is due on the 1st of each month (should be listed on the Rental Agreement as such), then he ought to make plans to mail the rent so it arrives by the 1st. Always be pleasant, but firm, and make the tenant aware that this is a basic business fundamental, nothing personal about it.

Remind him of his Agreement if necessary. If he seems not to understand why, remind him of the expenses, such as mortgage, taxes, the insurance, water, gas and electric, if you pay the utilities. Also there is your vital time to consider, which could expand to be considerable, if you don't limit this bad-behavior now. Hopefully, you're not too late, and the tenant pays the rent at that time. If he does not, proceed to step # 4.

–USE THE PROMISE LETTER–.

STEP 4. (around day 5) Use the promise letter if the tenant does not have the rent. A copy of the promise letter is found on page116, and it reaffirms that the tenant not only owes the rent, but plans to pay it. I usually will take a promise no further than the 15th of the same month, giving him approximately 10 to 12 more days to come up with the rent. If the tenant tells me that he cannot get the rent by the 15th, or he refuse to sign the promise letter, I give him a 3-day notice to vacate, which he does not have to sign. At that point, he will usually sign the promise letter then and there, to take advantage of the extra days instead of just 3 days. If the tenant does not sign, and take the 3-day notice, go to step 6. If he signed the promise letter, proceed to step 5.

–SECOND MEETING WITH TENANT–.

STEP 5 (around day 15) Make sure you are back to collect the rent on the date agreed upon. Check the time and place and firm it up so the tenant cannot claim some scheduling misunderstanding. These are important steps, as the tenant will know that you mean business, and possibly pay as required. If the tenant still has no rent, explain that you have tried to be fair and have given him every opportunity short of hurting your business, but now you have no choice but to ask him to move. Proceed to step 6.

–3-DAY NOTICE TO VACATE–.

STEP 6. (around days 5 thru 15) Give the tenant a 3-day notice to vacate. A copy of this form can be found on page 117. It indicates the reason you are giving him only 3 days to move. If the tenant fails to meet you at the appointed time, attach the 3-day notice to his door and mail him a copy of it by certified mail.

–FILE A PETITION OF EVICTION–.

STEP 7. (around days 9 thru 18) File a Petition of Eviction at the local Town Hall or wherever is appropriate in your particular city or town. Normally, the tenant will be given between 5 and 12 working days to appear in court. You will have to get someone over 18 years of age to serve this petition and notarize that they did so. If you have a problem executing service, the Sheriff or Marshal will serve it for a small fee. You will be obligated to notify the court if you collect the rent before the trial date. Be careful about accepting partial rents, because it may require you to go through the same time, trouble, and expense to re-file the petition to collect the balance of that rent. Eviction procedures will be covered in the next chapter.

–*Court Date*–.

STEP 8. (around days 20 thru 30) Go to court, and be on time. Have the Rental Agreement, promise letter, the 3-day notice, and any other written material that may be applicable. Provided your paperwork is in order, you do not have to worry about going to court; the burden of proof will be on the tenant. Often you will not have to say a word, except to identify yourself as the owner.

The Judge will sometime ask the tenant if he lives at the address on the petition and if he has paid the rent. Obviously, if he had paid, you would not be there, but if he says "yes", the Judge will ask him for proof or a written receipt. If he says "no", the Judge will ask him if he has the rent plus your expenses. If he has the money, everyone is happy, you get your rent, the court has done its job, all fees are taken care of, and the tenant gets to stay. After this unfortunate learning experience for him, the tenant should know better the next time, and most likely avoid this embarrassment by paying on time.

If the tenant does not have the money, the Judge will probably ask if there are any small children. Lack of children usually means a warrant of eviction immediately, but if small children are involved, it may require more time at the discretion of the Judge, sometimes a couple of weeks. The Judge may also make the tenant pay for any additional time that the tenant may need to vacate the premises.

–*Serve Eviction Notice*–.

STEP 9. (time period at Judge's discretion) If the tenant does not move after you have been issued the warrant of eviction, get the Sheriff or Marshal to handle it. He will first serve the tenant with a 72 hours' notice in person, if no one is home he will utilize a "Substitute of Service", which requires him to tack the notice to the door, and send the tenant a certified copy by mail. This notice will explain to the tenant that he is in illegal possession of the premises, and that at the end of 72 hours his personal property, belongings, along with any other persons occupying the property will be physically removed.

Most tenants' by this point will either have paid the rent or found another place to live. The tenant knows he doesn't have a leg to stand on, and to stay means being put out on the streets and his personal belongings being removed and stored at an additional expense. If the tenant is still there, we have one last and final step.

--Owner Gets Possession Of The Property--.

STEP 10. (approximately another 3 or 4 days after service) The Sheriff or Marshal will arrive, and you can have a moving truck available. Note that at this point the Sheriff or the Marshal has no discretion, they cannot take the rent and they cannot instruct the owner to except the rent, even if the tenant comes up with it. The Judge has already ruled and the warrant of eviction has already been entered. The owner however can still accept the rent, which will serve to nullify the warrant, but keep in mind if you do except the rent or partial payment the whole procedure will have to be executed from the beginning to evict this tenant.

First, the Sheriff or the Marshal will demand that the tenant vacate the premises. If the tenant refuses, the police are summoned, and the tenant is taken into custody for not abiding by the court order. At that time the owner can take possession of the property and legally change the locks. You can instruct the movers to take the property away and place it in storage at your own expense.

Alternatively, you could leave the tenants personal property in the apartment for 30 days and be responsible for it, but either way you have to record each item. If the tenant requests the property back within the 30 days, you have to give it to him. I would not suggest storing the personal property in the apartment as you need to get it ready for re-renting.

Warrant and Judgement.

You have possibly heard the terms "Warrant and Judgement" used together in court a lot. You've probably heard the term, "the Judge issued the warrant" and "the Judgement was entered in favor of the landlord". But what does it all mean? If the warrant issues, it means that possession of the apartment goes back to the landlord, most times immediately. If this happens the tenant must vacate the property immediately, if not the landlord will have to get the Sheriff or Marshal to complete the eviction.

You might have heard the Warrant was "stayed". What? It doesn't imply that the tenant gets to stay forever; it simply means that there is a hold on the "warrant of eviction". Usually this means that a Judge for some reason gave the tenant a "particular date" to pay an "exact amount". For example, the Judge could tell the tenant that he has 10 days to pay $1,000.00. If the tenant pays he can continue in possession of the apartment and the warrant dies, if not the warrant is issued and the tenant must move. Judges sometime fall for those sad stories too, when they do, they cut the tenant some slack.

The judgement only means that the Judge ruled that the tenant owes money to the landlord. The Judge will decide the amount, but the tenant now legally owes it. Now, go try to collect it.

How To Treat Partial Rent Payments.

You might ask, "what must I do if a tenant pays partial rent payments every month?" Well, there are a couple of choices. You can discourage this type of behavior by imposing stiff late charges. If that does not work, you can stop it completely by using the "SYSTEM".

You don't have to accept a partial rent payment. You can tell the tenant that you will not, and treat him as though he didn't have any of the rent at all. Start at Step #1 of the System and follow through. You don't need these problems, and you don't have to put up with them.

It's almost imperative (especially, if it's a new tenant) that you "nip it in the bud". It is very important that you handle this situation properly, because it may determine the pay pattern for the full term of his tenancy. Make him aware that it is a poor beginning. Make sure he understands the Rental Agreement, and determine if the due date is satisfactory. Any type of default on the first, second, or third rental payments calls for fast and decisive action.

Of course, if it is a long term tenant, who usually pays on time, handle it a little more patiently. A good tenant deserves some consideration when he has a problem, provided he doesn't make it a habit.

Some tenants may get paid only twice a month and may need some adjustment. If you're alright with it, make the arrangements. Make sure the tenant understand the exact pay dates, and follow through. Give each pay period the same amount of attention and scrutiny as you would any other rent payments.

Accomplishments Of "The SYSTEM".

Let's see just what has happened using the "SYSTEM". The tenant didn't pay the rent for the month, the tenant was evicted most likely the same month (or at the beginning of the next month), and now you can use the Security Deposit as the last month's rent. Provided there was little or no damage done, you could get a month's rent and a Security Deposit from another tenant on the first of the following month. You can begin advertising as soon as you get the warrant of eviction. Instead of letting month after month go by with a delinquent tenant not paying you, why not step up to the pump and remedy the situation immediately.

In my situation at the time I had to have a system that would give me confidence, a system that wouldn't miss. I was working a full-time job to make a living when I perfected this system, I did not have time to waste. You too should be vigilant to keep your business fervent, and lose the least amount of time and money as possible. Do it right from the beginning, and put in the necessary work to keep your business profitable.

The Owner Has The Upper-Hand with the "SYSTEM".

Word travels fast, and when the tenants know you mean business, they will usually either pay or leave. A tenant that intends to live rent-free will avoid you like the plague. You see, you have the upper hand, and you can be a nightmare to this type tenant, making him "pay to stay". You have to be firm in dealing with some tenants; I say again, the ground-rules are important.

Once I purchased a property that had a tenant living in it, that I had used the system on previously. The seller was having problems collecting the rent. After closing I went to the property, the tenant open the door, saw me, and yelled back to his wife "baby, we have to move".

As a matter of course, I personally collect at least the first three months' rent from a new tenant as it becomes due. Then, if there are no problems, I will allow the tenant to mail the rent to me. Your attitude should be that the tenant legally owes you the rent if he stays, and you can't afford not to get it.

NOTE$

CHAPTER 9

10
EVICTION DAY

COLLECTION STRATEGIES FOR THE REAL ESTATE OWNER,
LANDLORD, AND PROPERTY MANAGER.

Tenants In Property At The Time Of Purchase.

If you of having a problem, and have tried to work out the problems with a tenant that you have inherited through purchase, whatever the trouble may be, and you cannot resolve them, you might have to evict the tenant. There might be a regulation called "tenant rights", where you might have to give this tenant a little more consideration if they had arrangements with the old owner before you acquired the property. If the tenant is renting without a lease, on a month-to-month basis, typically you need only give them a 30 day notice to vacate. Although you could give this 30 day notice verbally, it is best to do it in writing.

The 30 day notice (NOTICE TO TERMINATE TENANCY) is found on page 118, and must correspond to the tenant's rental due date and give the tenant a full 30 days (Check with your Attorney for exact timing). In other words, if the tenant normally pays on the 1st of the month, he must receive the 30 day notice on or before the 1st of one month to be out by the 1st of the next month. If the tenant has a written lease agreement, you can ask him to leave by telling him that you will not be renewing his lease when it expires. You must give the tenant adequate notice of your intentions not to renew, as defined by the terms of the lease.

If you purchase a property and tenants are already there, you should have already inspected the condition of the apartment before closing, and know how well the tenant keeps it up. A look at the rental records should indicate if the tenant is behind in the rents. You might want to interview the tenant in person before you make a decision whether you want him to stay or leave.

If the tenant is not on a lease, you can send an introductory letter which can be seen on page 119. If you want the tenant to leave, send the 30 day notice. If the tenant is on a lease with the previous owner, you will have to abide by that lease (you should have inspected all applications, leases, and rental agreements before closing) but if you want the tenant to leave follow these steps. (1) send the introductory letter at closing; (2) send the tenant a letter two months (60 days) before the lease expires advising that you will not be renewing the lease, and that they should look for another place to stay; (3) send a 30 day notice one month before the lease expiration date.

Circumstances For 3-Day Notice.

If the tenant do not vacate by the 30 days, there are instances when the landlord can legally start eviction with a 3 day notice, this is one of those times (and especially with undesirable tenants). Sometime you have to be tough, and get respect, because you should recognize who you're dealing with, so save yourself a lot of time and trouble down the road. Listed here are some of the times when you'll want to use the 3 day notice;

#1. The tenant who has not paid the full amount of rent;

#2. The tenant is mildly destructive, noisy, or otherwise abusive of your rights or those of other tenants

#3. The tenant stays in the apartment beyond the time he is

supposed to leave. This tenant is sometimes referred to as a "hold-over"

Please note that the law only considers the things listed here as civil, but things that you may want to do to protect your property might be considered criminal. There are some things that you can and cannot do (these rules apply in my part of New York).

Among the things you cannot do is locking the tenant out (changing the locks) or removing his possession from the premises. You cannot turn off the tenant's utilities, or cause them to be turned off. You cannot harass the tenant beyond asking for your rent or asking him to leave.

There is something you can do if the tenant is destroying the property, however, you should waste no time in calling the police and initiating a court procedure known as a summary proceedings.

Obtain And Serve The Proper Documentation.

Before you start an eviction, call your local City Hall (and/or your Attorney) to check the procedure in your area. Usually to start an eviction action yourself, you must take the time to obtain and learn to fill out the proper documents that apply in your town or city. These forms, called "Notice of Petition", are inexpensive, and are usually available through any printer who specializes in legal documents. It is important that you complete both the fronts and the backs of these legal forms as thoroughly as possible. Some courts may require the date, time, and place the hearing will take place and how much money is involved if a judgement is sought.

You may also have to use a different form if you are evicting for non-payment of rent as opposed to evicting for other reasons. The Court Clerk or the Housing Council is a good place to get free help in filling out and filing the eviction forms. If you prefer, any attorney should be able to assist you for a fee. You must file these forms with the civil branch of the appropriate City or Town Hall.

In some places, it's your responsibility to have someone serve the tenant with these forms and it must be done within a particular time frame in accordance with the court schedule, so ask the Clerk. You cannot serve the papers on the tenant yourself, but anyone else who is over 18 years of age, not related to you, in their right mind, and not a party to the action may do so.

You may also employ a City Marshal or Sheriff to serve the papers for a small fee. The person who serves the forms may be required to fill out an affidavit of service depicting the physical description of the person served, the manner in which the papers were served, and his signature must be notarized on the affidavit.

Whenever possible, service should be by personal delivery to the tenant, especially if you will be asking the court to award you a judgment for any money the tenant owes you. If the papers cannot be personally delivered, "Substitute of Service" is permissible. That is, the papers can be given to anyone else who lives or works at the premises, provided the person is of suitable age and his description is recorded.

Another form of "Substitute of Service" involves posting a copy of the papers in a conspicuous place at the premises, usually on the entrance door (check with your attorney). With either type of substitute of service, a second copy of the papers served must be sent to the tenant by certified or registered mail within one day of the initial service. If you use substitute service and want to get a money judgment against the tenant, you must prove, in court that you tried repeatedly to have the papers served in person.

What Happens In Court.

When you go to court, it is important that you be there at the date and time specified. Take with you any supporting documentation you think you may need. For instance, you should bring copies of the eviction papers, a copy of the lease or rental agreement, any bills for damages done by the tenant, etc. The Judge will hear the case and decide whether to issue a Warrant of Eviction, and/or a money Judgement ordering the tenant to pay you rent and expenses, or both.

NOTE: This will only happen if your timing and papers are right, if not, the Judge will through your case out, and you will have to start over.

If the warrant of eviction is ordered, it is the tenant's duty to remove his possessions within the time the Judge allots. If the tenant does not vacate, you can pay a Marshal and a moving company (to pack and hall the tenant's personal property away) or store the property yourself.

You must also understand that you cannot use the eviction process to retaliate against a tenant because he has complained to the authorities about the conditions in his apartment, participated in a tenants' organization, or otherwise exercised his legal rights. If a tenant believes that your eviction attempt is retaliatory, he can contest it in court, and you will have to prove that you have a legal reason for wanting him out.

How To Locate A Tenant.

Let's assume that you went to court and the Judge awarded you both the warrant of eviction and a monetary judgement. Let's also assume that the tenant moved out (so you saved that expense) as directed by the court, but he owes you money for back rent and damages. Now, you want to locate the tenant. I don't know how much good it will do you, but there are some things you can do to locate him. Most people can be found by using the proper approach and investigating techniques quickly before the trail gets cold.

Below I have listed 32 good leads you can check. You must be very persistent to find a person, if he doesn't want to be found. When you make contact with anyone, you must make good inquiries to develop other leads. In your investigation, you must develop, and record relevant information to increase your chances of locating the tenant.

Follow the list in the order that it is arranged. It should give you the fastest results. Also ask for the tenant by nickname or any aliases you might know.

1. Try tenant's phone #; if new # is furnished, ask operator for the address as well
2. Ask the tenant's Telephone Company for information
3. Phone tenant's mother, father, relatives
4. Phone Spouse's mother, father, relatives
5. Phone employer (both tenant and spouse's)
6. Phone any other references in your file as well as on your application
7. Send a letter to the tenant at last address (might have put in a change of address)
8. Send letter to relatives, references, and employer
9. Call the Department of Motor Vehicles if you know his plate #
10. Call the Bank if you have his account #
11. Call the finance company where his car was financed
12. Check Post Office, file a "freedom of information" for new address
13. Personal contact with the neighbors
14. Personal contact with employer (tenant and spouse's)
15. Interview fellow employees of tenant and spouse
16. Check Employment and Bond Applications for leads
17. Personal contact with any Credit Unions
18. Personal contact with references for leads
19. Check tenant's old address, landlords, and neighbors
20. Interview the movers if you know who they are
21. Check with the kids school, teachers, records, other kids
22. Contact local gas stations, garages, grocery stores, and barber shops
23. Interview the dealership where tenant purchased his car
24. Check any clubs and organizations the tenant belongs to
25. Check with any creditors listed on your application

26. Check with tenant's insurance agent
27. Check with local Police
28. Check local bars and clubs
29. Check hospitals
30. Check local trailer rental companies
31. Check with the credit bureau
32. Check with the tenant's Attorney
33. Advertise in the newspaper (just kidding -I said 32 good leads above)

You got enough yet? All these leads could put you in a position to locate the tenant, but you still have to collect. The best time to collect is, well, you know. That's a lot of work, and it might turn out to be a wild goose chase anyway, why not spend the time trying to buy your next property or locating a good tenant.

What Questions To Ask.

OK, if you insist on finding this tenant anyway, whenever you make a contact on the list above don't just ask, "Do you know where he moved to?" or "do you know where I can find him?" You need to ask probing questions.

EXAMPLE OF PROBING QUESTIONS:

FRIENDS AND NEIGHBORS – When talking to friends and neighbors, you could ask such questions as where does the wife work (phone them), where does the children go to school (personal contact or phone them), was tenant involved with any welfare or charitable organizations, does he frequent bars (phone or stop by for interview), what hobbies or other past times he had (fishing, swimming, horse racing fan, boating, target shooting, pool shark, golf hustler, etc.), where would he likely appear to perform these events. Does he need a license or permit for any of these activities. Do you know any other family members, or other friends?

EMPLOYERS – When talking to employers you may want to ask if the tenant had any special qualification (profession that might require membership or license). Also find out if he had any friends working there, if there are references listed on his employment application, and was money being taken out and sent to anyone else.

CREDITORS – When dealing with creditors, you could ask if they have a new address for the tenant, what references do they show on their application, who is the Co-signer on their loan, as well as where the tenant may have live before.

PREVIOUS LANDLORDS – If speaking with a former landlord, check his application if possible for any other pertinent information, where the tenant lived before he moved there, was he friends with any of the tenant at this location, and their kids might know his kids. I might note that the information you receive will possibly be more trustworthy than if you were inquiring in order to rent an apartment to this tenant. It's not unheard of for a current landlord to lie and say this is a great person (with his fingers crossed of course), to get rid of a bad tenant.

AUTOMOBILE DEALER – In your conversation with the auto dealer and salesperson, find out who brought the tenant in for his deal, did tenant bring anybody else in, does the records show a new phone number for the tenant, where did tenant purchase his previous car, and where was the tenant employed at that time?

While making inquiries get the correct spelling, street address, phone number, business locations, and any other leads that may help you uncover information. It will take a great deal of time and effort to check all the potential leads mentioned above, but you must stay with it if you are serious about locating your tenant.

If you get to the end of the list and you still haven't found him, start from the beginning and re-contact all the leads again for something which you may have missed or new information that might have been obtained since your last contact.

It is not unheard of to offer a small cash reward if you want the tenant bad enough, although I advise against it.

_____

_____

_____

_____

_____

_____

_____

_____

_____

_____

_____

_____

_____

_____

_____

_____

_____

_____

_____

11

REFLECTING ON HOW RENTAL PROPERTY WORKS

COLLECTION STRATEGIES FOR THE REAL ESTATE OWNER,
LANDLORD, AND PROPERTY MANAGER.

Your Future With Real Estate.

I would like to take this opportunity to thank you for having the insight to purchase this book. The fact that you did proves that you are serious about your future with real estate. That future may depend on your knowing how to collect, your ability to understand a given situation, take full control, and work skillfully toward a favorable end. Remember, you are your own boss with real estate, so don't get lazy. You'll have to be a self-starter.

For those of you who have been in real estate awhile, you may already know the proven concepts that I outline in this chapter. I strongly encourage you to re-read and use "The System" as explained in chapter 9. It has been my experience, and I truly believe that you will get the best results with the least amount of time and trouble when you use the "The System".

For the beginning investor it is essential that you believe and act according to the concepts and advice that follows. A tenant's failure or neglect to fulfill his obligation should not be allowed to stop your progress. Visualize in your mind the different collection situations that may occur until they become an unconscious adjustment of your behavior. In our land of great opportunity, you can take the road to wealth that has been proven over and over again. You don't have to re-invent the wheel, just follow the simple rules for success in this chapter.

About taking A Chance.

Just like in any other endeavor, sometimes you take a chance and bad things happen, sometimes you take a chance and good things happen. But with real estate for sure, if you don't take a chance, nothing happens. Prepare yourself properly if you take the chance, then you give yourself a better than average chance of success, and thus the good things are more likely to happen for you.

While considering a business opportunity, a lady was trying to decide if she should take a chance on what was being taught in the class. She said to one of the instructors "if I do it, I'll be 40 years old by the 2 years' time it's going to take me to get my company up and running". The instructor looked at her and asked, "how old will you be in 2 years, if you don't?" Chances are, if you are looking for an excuse not to, you probably won't take a chance.

By the way if you want to enhance your chances of success, avail yourself of one of the great institutions of higher learning (college). Do not make the foolish mistake of getting addicted to such things as alcoholic beverages, using wacky weed, taking drugs, or the like.

How The System Restored My Trust.

What you read in Chapter 9 "The System" was made possible for me, because of my willingness and steadfastness to learn how to get a court ordered for an eviction within about a month. I had to learn how to get an eviction myself because I once used an attorney when a tenant wouldn't pay the $500.00 rent they owed. I tried to be as nice as I could to this tenant, but my power of persuasion was failing me miserably and I felt a sense of hopelessness.

Mistake #1. It took three months to make the decision to evict. Mistake #2. I was taking promise, after promise, after promise. Mistake #3. The attorney I used took another three months to effect the eviction and charged me almost $400.00. Do the math, 6 months of $500.00 lost rent, $400.00 attorney fee, a marshal fee, a moving charge, clean out, repairs that took almost a month, and the advertising fee it took for another month to get the property re-rented.

Ask yourself; was it worth it to learn how to evict myself? The fee was only about $40.00 for me to file the papers at the Court. I say if you going to be in the business, you have to learn how to do the business. Learning how to evict a tenant was imperative; and it was that tool, that led me to develop "The System", with great trial and error of course. These were the foundations of my success in Real Estate; they were born out of necessity. I already knew how to collect and manage, so after I found out how to buy right, I was on my way.

Learning the Eviction Procedure.

In my case it was an experience, the first time I tried to get an eviction, I went to the Housing Counsel, read all I could, listen to a lot of advice, and got the necessary papers together. When I arrived in court the Judge dismissed my case for some small paperwork issue and told me I had to start over. Again I re-filed, served the papers and the Judge found another small discrepancy with my papers that was also on that first petition, so I asked the Judge why he didn't point out the error when I was there last time. The Judge told me that he was not my attorney, and that it was not his job to help with my case (even though he could clearly see that the tenant was taking advantage of me).

I went through the process again, dotted all the I's, crossed all the

T's, and made all the corrections. I remember the anticipation in that court room when the Judge took his time looking over all my paper-work, twice, front and back. He looked at me, he looked at the ten-ant, and then he looked back at me and said "you got the eviction".

I can't tell you how happy I was, not because I was doing some-thing against that tenant, no, this had greater implications. I had just saved my Real Estate business! I do not think that I would have sur-vived letting the tenant stay months for free and paying high attorney's fees.

After giving some serious thought about the legal system here in New York, I concluded that Judges have kids who are attorneys, and they need the business.

Get Knowledgeable.

In the interest of staying with the subject matter of collection Strategies, I have only touched on some of the other important phases of Real Estate. In other words I have given you just the "meat" of the business. You will still need some potatoes, soup and bread to make a well-rounded meal. If you have not taken one of the many Real Estate Courses available, please do so. That is how I got started.

You will need to know many other things about Real Estate ac-quisitions than what is contained in this writing if you are a beginner and plan to be successful and stay in the business very long. Things like locating the right property, sizing up the seller, how much the property is worth, leverage, negotiation, writing a purchase offer, tax consequences, trading properties, choosing a Realtor, a Lawyer, when to close, and much, much more are all areas you need to become knowledgeable in. It is said that knowledge is power, so I have in-cluded below a list of books written by some of the world's foremost motivation personalities and experts on Real Estate.
BOOKS AND TAPES

FINANCIAL GENIUS   - - MARK O. HAROLDSEN

Join a Landlord Organization

Associate yourself with a group that are dedicated to the support of landlords like The New York State Coalition of Property Owners and Businesses, Inc. " An Organization for the rights of the people ". I was elected to this Associations Board of Directors, and personally helped many Landlords with many problems myself.

The Mission Statement of the New York State Coalition is; "We believe, united together, through our vast resources, mounds of experience within our membership base, and through educational forums -- we can assist, help, guide, and inform on all areas of property ownership, so that you can achieve your real estate investment goals.

We also believe that personal property rights are the foundation of this success and are an important part of becoming a professional, responsible (business) property owner – therefore the Coalition maintains a high awareness of proposed legislation, case law and statutory laws that affect our business and when necessary use the judicial system to provide relief and positive change for all".

This particular organization is located in Rochester New York, but try to find one near you and get involved. You do not know everything, so realize that vast amounts of wisdom, expertise, and resources can be uncovered there, which will be of great help to you in running your real estate business.

Set A Goal.

There was an exchange between Alice and the Cheshire Cat (Alice in Wonderland) that said, "If you don't know where you are going, any road will take you there". I interpret this to mean when you get to the end of that road you will arrive at some place, where you <u>don't know where you are</u>. This place could be good or this place could be bad. Don't take that chance. Set a goal, plan your course of action, and proceed toward that goal.

Albert Einstein said Insanity is doing the same thing over and over again and expecting different results. If your rational is like this fellow who went on his first doctor's appointment, you might not appreciate Einstein. The Doctor said "I see in the records that your family suffers from severe mental illness", and he said "noooo, no sir, we enjoy it very much". If that's you, put down the book slowly, back away and go get yourself a Popsicle. But let me be earnest, I believe there's hope if you've read this far.

You might be saying nothing goes right for me, it might be your words and actions that are the problem, just change your actions. Take a different direction, and start doing right things instead. Set your goals to get proven desired results.

Choose your words carefully, don't just easy speak, and don't constantly say things that are negative. Talk about the positive things you want in life. An old pastor told me that words are like containers, they're going somewhere to happen. He said "speak those things that be not (the things you want) as though they were (like you already got it)", and you will have them. I like this saying, and it works well for me.

Know Where You Are Going.

Any one of the sources listed above will give you direction and get you started on your business venture straight toward your goals. These real estate authors may use different systems, but all seem to work well because it's the nature of real estate itself that's really important. You just need the right direction, and then get started. I read somewhere that everybody should own at least one piece of investment property.

The theory is that in the long run, even if you didn't make one penny per month, even if the property didn't increase one penny in value, and even if you didn't take advantage of all the great tax deductions each year – You would have invested with a low or no down payment, the rental income would have paid it off over the years, and you would have the benefit of the full value of that property in your portfolio free and clear.

While you are setting goals and deliberating about where you are going, reflect on the long term consequences of your words and actions as well. There is another serious question I would suggest that you ask yourself "where will I spend eternity?" Remember our topic "Know Where You Are Going".

Get Motivated And Take Action.

These great authors also provide the motivation that is essential. All is in vain, if they give you a road map, but can't get you to take the trip. You must have a need, both conscious and unconscious, that incites a person to action. To change your position in life, you are to get that extra drive, that propelling behavior that will generate the power for you to harvest your own financial independence. After taking one of these courses, just remember you have got to act.

Just "know how" alone, will not make you rich. Some people will take many real estate courses, have a wealth of knowledge, and be capable of carrying on an intelligent conversation with the experts, but never acquire the courage to purchase one property. Some of these people are the most educated, poverty-stricken people you ever seen. If knowledge is power, then action must be the key. Nothing happens without action. Hopefully, this book has taken away some of the mysteries, and other unknowns you might have had. I'd say "Go for it".

It may take a little time, I heard about this man who was praying for patience, he was saying all the right things, but at the end he said "and God I want it right now". Sometime you may have to employ patience, and build up to the right time, slow growth is good growth.

NOTE$

CHAPTER 11

12
FINAL WORDS

COLLECTION STRATEGIES FOR THE REAL ESTATE OWNER,
LANDLORD, AND PROPERTY MANAGER.

Formulate The Successful Outlook.

Statistics say you will not get rich working for someone else, and most new businesses fail within the first three years. Some people don't even like their jobs, but they will not quit, they work as little as possible to get that check, but just hard enough so they won't get fired. They seem to be stuck, right, and they know if they stay in that old job they are sure not going to get rich. If they leave and try to start their own business, statistics are against them.

So, it looks bad, right? Wrong! Real Estate is not like most businesses. As a matter of fact, the largest percent of all new millionaires make their fortunes through real estate. Also, in real estate you don't have to quit your job until you want to. You can do it in your spare time, as I did.

Look, I have nothing against the stock market, gold, or silver investing, heck I even own some myself, but they didn't make me independent from my job like real estate did. With these other investments someone else gets to decide the price, and it may go down without your consent, and there's nothing you can do about it. And even if it goes up, you can't get anyone to pay you rent for it month after month, or get that appreciation tax break without doing anything extra. I think the people who make the laws in this country must own some Real Estate.

I would like to convey an important concept before I finish, and submit to you, that real estate is the exception to the rule. The rule says "you work an hour, you get paid for an hour", "Work eight hours, and get paid for eight hours". The rules thus implies that in order to get paid for another eight hours, you must work another eight hours. But, through real estate you could spend eight hours working to purchase an income producing property and literally get paid for that same eight hours (through rent collections) for as long as you desire. Think about it, rules, no rules, this is exceptional.

There's Value In Owning.

In one of the seminars I went to, someone said "stop working hard for the money and let the money work hard for you". This reminds me of when I met a Realtor that I had purchased properties from about ten years earlier, and he made a comment "it's going", which summed up his feelings that day. Through that whole conversation I was thinking "yes, but it's really going great for me", but I didn't say that to him.

I remember back then he spent a lot of time going through a lot of property and showing it, and talking other people into buying and selling. I guess he was happy every time he got that possible $2,000.00 to $6,000.00 commission. That's not bad, but if you think about it when one closing was done and he received the check, what did he have to do to get paid again? You know the answer, back to that 9 to 5 grind.

After my talk with the Realtor I realized that I was still getting paid every month from some of the properties that he had sold to me. He didn't see the value of owning, but that's OK, we need somebody to find these great deals for us.

You need knowledge to be successful and there are two ways to get it; (1) by trial and error or (2) by the experiences of others. I would like to suggest the latter in this particular instance because every error may cost you thousands or even hundreds of thousands of dollars. Take it from me, and get educated about real estate, become an active expert in the field and you will prosper.

On A Serious Note.

Find God if you want true satisfaction and peace. You need to know that God is a Good God. I always wanted to start out a story like this, so here we go. "Once upon a time", there was a poor old lady and an evil neighbor. This neighbor thought he would trick the old lady by buying groceries, sitting them by her front door and when she would thank God, he would tell her "I paid for that grocery". So it felt like his plan was working, and he was eager to see the disappointment in her face, but when he told her, she started to praise the Lord even louder. He could not believe what he was hearing, so he said "didn't you hear me; I told you I bought the grocery? And she look up and said "I thank you God, not only did you provide the grocery that I so desperately needed, but you got the devil to pay for it.

There was a young man going on and on about his Grandmother, "how she was a great woman of God, how she went to Church all the time, how she helped so many people, etc." The minister asked him "what about you"? In that conversation it was revealed to this young man that God does not have any Grandkids, only sons and daughters. You have to know God for yourself, so seek the way, the truth and the life.

Be a giver because as the principal goes, that's how you get. Find a Church that believes and is doing good works; get involved and pay tithe (give a 10th).

I can't explain all the integral details for you, but when God says you can do it and you truly believe, you do it. Then it will work for you, and you will have good success. Be a cheerful giver. Give your time, talent and treasure, find a good place to volunteer these things, if you want to be happy and live a fulfilling life.

Don't be deceived and don't be put in Bondage. I had a tenant once who would go out and get a Church in the community to pay the rent for her, each month a different Church. Then when they stopped paying she called a large TV ministry to pay a month's rent for her. I had to confirm by phone the situation to get the rent. I was a giver to this TV ministry, and still give today. The lady on the phone with the TV ministry wanted to know "how could I be a Christian" when I had threatened to evict this tenant.

I got the rent, but I was in bondage because of her words. I had to meet with my pastor before I could feel good about myself again. It was a confirmation for me, and truly liberating when he believed in me and spoke these words "that he could see that I ran a legitimate business, I was providing a needed service to reputable people in my community, and I was not the one trying to take advantage of others". I continued to give to the TV ministry, mainly because I was determine not to let that one statement deceive me enough, to stop supporting a group that was doing such great work all across the US and around the world.

Work a job. Real Estate could be it, but if not all is not lost, whatever profession you choose, do it with enthusiasm. The first man was given the responsibility to till the ground and tending the garden, his name was Adam. He had a job, before he had a wife. Find and start working a job, and be committed to that job, before you get your wife, because this puts it in the right order, and it's the right thing to do, even today. You can read all about it in the Bible, it corroborates the whole story about Adam and the beginning of everything.

Find a Wife (or Husband). God is the one who said "it is not good that the man should be alone". And it's said that if a man finds a wife, he finds a good thing, also it's implied that they should leave everyone else behind, and cleave unto one another. I would add also that the man will truly be blessed, if he finds, and I stress "a good wife, as I did when I found Loretta. My wife is a strong sturdy influence in my life. She helps me in every way, and is the ideal partner for life. A good wife is supposed to be a helper and stand by her husband through good times and bad. A man is supposed to love and protect his wife.

I heard a pastors wife say "you find them (a good wife) where they're at". This means you can find them where "they teach woman to love and be faithful to their husbands". That doesn't sound like the local bar to me, sounds like the church may be a more appropriate place to look. Remember, that behind every successful man, stands a woman "rolling her eyes", or something like that. Oh, wait, sorry about that, to be more accurate it seem that a successful man has - "a strong, wise and hardworking woman" standing with him. Oh, boy, that's good news.

General Advice.

I know this is just a real estate book, but would you allow me to be a little light hearted and offer some general advice about life? I think it's worthwhile to smile every now and then, while gaining knowledge.

Be a learner, a man was trying to tell this guy something, but the guy kelp insisting "I see it, I see it", and the man said "if you saw it, why did you step in it". You have to take a minute to consider what is being said.

Another thing, don't be condescending to people, you'll get a lot further in life. A friend related an incident to me that occurred when he was a young boy. He and his dad were walking into the Mall, and this fellow approached and said "hey Buddy, can you tell me where the Wal-Mart is", and his dad said "Nope". After the man left, my friend questioned his father's answer, and said "dad we just left the Wal-Mart", and his dad articulated, "if he is smart enough to know my name is Buddy, then he ought to be smart enough to know where the Wal-Mart is".

Don't always try to draw attention to yourself. I overheard a man talking about some things that happened when he was incarcerated. He noticed this little guy in the prison yard every day, and nobody would talk to him. This man asked another inmate why, and he was told "the little guy was in prison because he stole a fire truck, yea that's real intelligent; he tried to make his get away in a loud, big, red vehicle". That kind of attention we don't need.

Be patient and shrewd, wait, and don't be so fast to jump in. A man was in a crowded Supermarket and his friend saw him and yelled out "loan me $20.00", the man said "what did you say", and his friend hollered back "loan me $20.00", for which the man responded "what", and the person standing next to him, tapped him on the shoulder and said "your friend wants you to loan him $20.00", to which the man replied "you heard it, you loan it to him".

Don't think more highly of yourself than you ought to. Just like some people the Devil thinks he is great and awesome. One day the Devil was conversing with God and said "hey, I can make a man, it's simple, and all I have to do is to take some of this dirt" and God stopped him there, and said "wait a minute, you got to get your own dirt". We need to humble ourselves before God, because the fear of the Lord is the beginning of wisdom.

Last Words.

In one of the courses I took, they suggested that I go to a Realtor class, so that I would know what they know, and get familiar with real estate terms, so I did. They also suggested that I do not get my Realtor's License even though I would be qualified, because in New York you have to disclose that fact to all sellers and buyers.

You do not want to be seen as a Realtor (real estate expert) when you talk to sellers about buying their property, you want to be seen as just a plain ordinary guy. Seller's feel when a Real Estate Agent is involved in a deal, he should be finding them a deep pocket buyer, but we are trying to locate a deal. A Seller could possibly have suspicion that the price is much too low, if a Realtor is trying to purchase the property, and we don't want that.

I want to think God for letting me write these principals, and I believe that He'll let them work for anyone –including you. I consider this to be a self-help book but, you might want to refer to it by name "Collection Strategies by Eula C. Dozier". A man walked up to the Liberian and asked where the self-help books could be found, and she said "I could tell you, but that would defeat the purpose".

Whereas there is no legal advice, and no guarantees offered or intended in this book, I believe that you will find the concepts very workable. I strongly suggest that you check with your attorney because sometimes laws are changed or regulations and/or policies are deleted, withdrawn and/or overturned. You should review this book often. Whenever you have a tenant or collection problem, just go to the appropriate section of the book for a possible solution to the problem. Hope you took plenty of notes. Even after reading this book two or three times, you will probably still find information that you had forgotten.

Good Luck
And
May God Bless You!

Now - CUT OUT THE LAST PAGE, TYPE YOUR NAME AND DATE IN THE APPROPRIATE SPACES ON THE "CERTIFICATE OF ACHIEVEMENT", PUT IT IN A FRAME, THEN HANG IT ON A WALL IN PLAIN VIEW WHERE EVERYONE CAN SEE IT.

NOTE$

CHAPTER 12

APPENDIX—FORMS

POSTER OF

PERMISSION

IT IS BESTOWED UPON "YOU", THE BEARER OF THIS POSTER, PERMISSION TO COLLECT ALL RENTS DUE YOU.

YOU, THE BEAR, HAVE THE INALIENABLE RIGHT TO SEEK OUT, FIND, AND SOLVE ANY AND ALL PROBLEMS AS THEY RELATE TO MANAGEMENT OF YOUR PROPERTY.

YOU, THE BEARER, ARE EMPOWERED TO CONDUCT YOUR BUSINESS OF REAL ESTATE IN A SAFE AND PLEASANT MANNER.

YOU, THE BEARER, UPON CONSENT TO THE OBJECTIVE, WILL STUDY AND ACQUIRE THE KNOWLEDGE THAT WILL MAKE YOU SECURE.

YOU, THE BEARER, ARE PRESENTED THE AUTHORITY, IF IT IS YOUR DESIRE, TO BECOME SUCCESSFUL.

PROPERTY ANALYSIS

PROPERTY ANALYSIS

ASSESSOR _____   PROPERTY ADDRESS _____

Tax # _____   Assessed Value $_____

City Tax # _____
County Tax # _____
Water Bureau # _____ (Call for final reading)
Pure Water # _____
City Refuse # _____ (it applicable)

City True Tax	
Property	$_____
School	$_____
Embellishment	$_____
Refuse	$_____

$_____ Total Expenses per Year

divided by 12 = $_____ per month

CITY ZONING DEPARTMENT # _____   PROPERTY ZONED FOR _____

ITEM	DELINQUENT BILLS AMOUNT	PERIOD OR EXPLAINATION
_____	$_____	_____
_____	$_____	_____
_____	$_____	_____
_____	$_____	_____

Comments:

FIXED EXPENSES

| TAX YEAR | PROPERTY ADDRESS | CLOSING DATE |

Date "C of O" Ordered

Amount
$

Date Approved

Insurance Co.

Amount
$

Check #

Date Paid

County Tax
$

Date Due

Check #

Date Paid

CITY TAXES PAID

$ _____ Check # _____ Date Paid _____
$ _____ Check # _____ Date Paid _____
$ _____ Check # _____ Date Paid _____
$ _____ Check # _____ Date Paid _____

Water

$ _____ / _____ / _____
amount   check #   date

$ _____ / _____ / _____
amount   check #   date

$ _____ / _____ / _____
amount   check #   date

$ _____ / _____ / _____
amount   check #   date

$ _____ / _____ / _____
amount   check #   date

Pure Water

$ _____ / _____ / _____
amount   check #   date

$ _____ / _____ / _____
amount   check #   date

$ _____ / _____ / _____
amount   check #   date

$ _____ / _____ / _____
amount   check #   date

$ _____ / _____ / _____
amount   check #   date

COMMENTS:

Cash Flow Statistic

CASH FLOW STATISTIC

Section 1. (Property Information) ///

PROPERTY ADDRESS _____   AGENT _____

OWNER'S NAME _____   ADDRESS _____

OWNER'S ADDRESS _____   PHONE # _____

OWNER'S PHONE # _____   MORTGAGE BALANCE $ _____

MORTGAGE HOLDER _____   MONTHLY PAYMENT $ _____

ASKING PRICE $_____   MORTGAGE ASSUMABLE   YES / NO
                                              CIRCLE ONE

Section 2. (Income Information) ///

	CURRENT RENT	LOCATION AND BEDROOMS	PROJECTED RENT
Apt # 1.	$ _____	_____	$ _____
Apt # 2.	$ _____	_____	$ _____
Apt # 3.	$ _____	_____	$ _____
Apt # 4.	$ _____	_____	$ _____
TOTAL INCOME	$ _____		$ _____

Section 3. (Offer Information) //

1. $_____ $_____ $_____ at ___% for ___ = $_____ per month
      offer   down   seller mortgage   interest   years

2. $_____ $_____ $_____ at ___% for ___ = $_____ per month
      offer   down   seller mortgage   interest   years

3. $_____ $_____ $_____ at ___% for ___ = $_____ per month
      offer   down   seller mortgage   interest   years

Section 4. (Cost Information) //

	1st. Offer	2nd. Offer	3rd. Offer
BANK MORTGAGE	$_____	$_____	$_____
OWNER MORTGAGE	$_____	$_____	$_____
TAXES	$_____	$_____	$_____
INSURANCE	$_____	$_____	$_____
WATER	$_____	$_____	$_____
GAS	$_____	$_____	$_____
ELECTRIC	$_____	$_____	$_____
MAINTENANCE	$_____	$_____	$_____
TOTAL COST	$_____	$_____	$_____

Section 5. (Profit Information) ///

	1st Offer	2nd Offer	3rd Offer
INCOME	$_____	$_____	$_____
EXPENSE	$_____	$_____	$_____
CASH FLOW	$_____	$_____	$_____

RENTAL APPLICATION

RENTAL APPLICATION

Address of Property you are applying for: _____ Do You Have a Pet? Y / N -TYPE PET _____

Date you want to move in: _____ # BEDROOMS NEEDED: _____ # OF KIDS: _____

NAME: _____ AGE: _____

CURRENT ADDRESS: _____ PHONE #: _____

DATE OF BIRTH: _____ CURRENT RENT: $_____ HOW LONG THERE: _____ SOC SEC # _____

LANDLORD'S NAME, ADDRESS _____ PHONE #: _____

YOUR PRIOR ADDRESS: _____ HOW LONG THERE: _____

PRIOR LANDLORD'S NAME, ADDRESS, AND _____ PHONE #: _____

YOUR EMPLOYER: _____ ADDRESS: _____ WAGES $_____

YOUR POSITION: _____ SUPERVISOR'S NAME: _____ SUPERVISOR"S TITLE: _____

Circle one ------> DSS- Y / N   C.A.P - Y / N   SECTION 8 - Y / N   SOCIAL SECURITY OR SSI - Y / N

ASSISTANCE CLIENTS INFORMATION

WORKER'S NAME : _____ WORKER'S #: _____ CASE #: _____

Circle one ------> IS DSS RECOUPING MONEY FROM YOUR GRANT? Y / N   * VOUCHER RENT? FULL / PART / NO
HUSBAND/WIFE: _____ HIS/HER AGE: _____ LIVE WITH YOU? Y / N   ON YOUR GRANT ? Y / N
BOYFRIEND/GIRLFRIEND
HIS/HER EMPLOYER: _____ EMPLOYER PHONE #: _____ CURRENT INCOME: $_____

LIST OTHER PERSONS WHO WILL OCCUPY THE APARTMENT WITH YOU:

FULL NAME	AGE	RELATIONSHIP TO YOU	INCOME

EMERGENCY- Name: _____ Address: _____ Phone #: _____

References: List two people that you know personally and has phones numbers.

FULL NAME	ADDRESS	PHONE #

By signing this application I agree that any false statement made on this application will be grounds "not" to rent to me. If I have moved into the property when a false statement is discovered, it will be grounds to ask me to leave immediately without any further notice.

I have personally inspected the property and found it to be in "good condition" and it "meets with my needs and satisfaction".
DO NOT SIGN THIS APPLICATION IF ANY STATEMENT "IS FALSE" OR "NOT AGREEABLE" TO YOU!

Signature _____ Date: _____

LEASE

LEASE AGREEMENT

When signed, this document becomes a binding contract.

The Landlord and Tenant agree to lease the Premises at the rental amount and for the term stated below:

LANDLORD:	TENANT:
_____	_____
_____	_____
_____	_____
Phone: _____	Phone: _____

Premises: _____

Lease date:	Term: _____	Yearly Rent $ _____
	Beginning _____	Monthly Rent $ _____
_____	Ending _____	Security Deposit $ _____
		Pet Deposit $ _____

1. Use

The Premises must be used to live in only and for no other reason. Only a party signing the Lease, spouse and children of that party may use the Premises.

2. Failure to give possession

Landlord shall not be liable for failure to give Tenant possession of the Premises on the beginning date of the Term. Rent shall be payable as of the beginning of the Term unless Landlord is unable to give possession. In that case, rent shall be payable when possession is available. Landlord will notify Tenant as to the date possession is available. The ending date of the Term will not change unless property conditions becomes unusable long-term for acts of God or other reasons not covered in this lease.

3. Rent, added rent

The rent payment for each month must be paid on the eighteenth day of that month at Landlord's Address above. Landlord need not give notice to pay the rent. Rent must be paid in full and no amount subtracted from it. The first month's rent is to be paid when Tenant signs this Lease. Tenant may be required to pay other charges to landlord under terms of this Lease. They are to be called "added rent." This added rent is payable as rent, together with the next monthly rent due. If Tenant fails to pay the added rent on time, Landlord shall have the same rights against Tenant as if it were failure to pay rent.

The whole amount of rent is due and payable when this Lease is effective. Payment of rent in installments is for Tenant's convenience only. If Tenant defaults, Landlord may give notice to Tenant that Tenant may no longer pay rent in installments. The entire rent for the remaining part of the Term will then be due and payable.

Rental payments received 6 days after rent is due are subject to a penalty equal to 5% of the monthly rent ($25.00 minimum), payments not received after 10 days are subject to an additional $25.00 administrative charge plus $1.00 a day there after. Any monies received after charges are incurred shall be applied first to the late and administrative charges and the remainder toward current month's rent. Late Charges are added rent and becomes due and payable on the dates accrued.

4. Notices

Any bill, statement or notice must be in writing and delivered or mailed to the Tenant at the Premises and to the Landlord at the Address for notices. It will be considered delivered on the day mailed or if not mailed, when left at the proper address. Any notice must be sent by certified mail. Landlord must send Tenant written notice if Landlord changes the Address for Notices. Tenant must notify Landlord of any inspection requested by the tenant, and inform anyone requesting an inspection of the property, to arrange dates and times of that inspection with the Landlord.

5. Security   **Pick one below** ///// Sec Deposit   -paid   or   -not?   /////

Tenant has not paid a Security Deposit to Landlord.

Or

Tenant has given Security to Landlord in the amount stated above. If Tenant fully complies with all Terms of this Lease, Landlord will return the Security after the term ends. If Tenant does not fully comply with the terms of this Lease, Landlord may use the Security to pay amounts owed by Tenant, including damages. If Landlord sells the Premises, Landlord may give the Security to the buyer. Tenant will only look to the buyer for the return of the Security.

6. Utilities and services

The Tenant is responsible for the services checked below: Tenant will pay any usage, fines and/or fees regardless of whose name appear on the bill.

SHARED METER CONDITIONS (75 kilometer –more or less): The rental amount on page one of this agreement reflects all compensation due to the tenant, and is the adjusted rental balance due to the owner.

☐ GAS	☐ TELEPHONE	☐ SNOW REMOVAL
☐ ELECTRIC	☐ WATER	☐ LAWN CARE
☐ FUEL	☐ SEWER	☐ ALARM SERVICE
☐ EXTERMINATING	☐ CABLE	☐ TRASH REMOVAL
☐ OTHER	☐ OTHER:	☐ OTHER:

7. Furnishings

If the Premises are furnished, the furniture and other furnishings are accepted "as is." If an inventory is supplied each party shall have a signed copy.

8. Repairs, alterations, carpeting

Tenant must keep, and, at the end of the Term, return, the Premises and all appliances, equipment, furniture, furnishings and other personal property clean and in good order and repair. Tenant is not responsible for ordinary wear and damage by the elements. If Tenant defaults, Landlord has the right to make repairs and charge Tenant the cost. The cost will be added rent. Tenant must not alter, decorate, change or add to the Premises. If there is wall to wall carpet, Tenant will have the carpet cleaned within 5 days prior to vacating the premises. Tenant shall be responsible for all minor repairs and replacement, and shall make these repairs in a timely manner.

9. Space "as is"

Tenant has inspected the Premises. Tenant states that the property is in good order and repair and accepts the Premises "as is." Tenant agrees to pay for any additional material and/or labor cost (including Lead Paint removal) that he/she feels would improve his/her families own living conditions at the property.

10. Care of Premises, grounds, vehicles, parking

Tenant shall keep grounds neat and clean. Parking shall be as indicated below. The tenant agrees to pay for damages (including for plugged drains) to the apartment that occurs during his/her term only. Tenant shall replace broken glass of windows. The tenant agrees not to paint or make any alterations to the property without written permission from the owner. The tenant is responsible for, and shall take care of the apartment during their occupancy and agrees to keep the property clean inside and outside. The tenant shall maintain the Smoke Detector in operable condition and replace Smoke Detector Batteries as needed. The tenant will maintain the premises (including hallways, stairs, windows, doors, garage, yard, etc.) in a reasonable and habitable condition, and remove any particles that contain Lead Paint. The tenant will be responsible for snow removal, lawn mowing, leaves, garbage containers, and removal of any garbage or debris accumulated at the premises. On the morning of, or the night before pickup, garbage will be sat on the curb and properly bundled by the tenant. The tenant will pay for all Garbage Code Violations. After the first 60 day period the tenant will be responsible for Roach, Insect, and Rat Extermination.

☐ GARAGE	☐ COMMON LOT	☐ ON STREET ONLY
☐ DRIVEWAY	☐ ASSIGNED SPACE #___	☐ NO PARKING

Vehicles may not be parked or driven on lawn. All vehicles must be licensed.

11. Fire, damage

Tenant must give Landlord immediate notice in the case of fire or other damage to the Premises. Landlord will have the right to repair the damage within a reasonable time or cancel this Lease. If Landlord elects to make repairs, the Tenant shall pay rent only to the date of fire or damage and shall start to pay rent again when the Premises becomes usable. Landlord may cancel the Lease by giving Tenant three (3) days' written notice. The Term shall be over at the end of the third day and all rent shall be paid to the date of the damage.

12. Liability

Landlord is not liable for loss, expense or damage to any person or property of others. Tenant must pay for damages suffered and money spent by Landlord relating to any claim arising from any act or neglect of Tenant. Tenant is responsible for all acts of Tenant's family, employees, guests and invitees.

13. Landlord's consent

If Tenant requires Landlord's consent to any act and such consent is not given, Tenant's only right is to ask the Court to force the Landlord to give consent. Tenant agrees not to make any claim against Landlord for money or subtract any sum from rent because such consent was not given. All consent must be in writing.

14. Assignment, sublet

Tenant may not sublet all or part of the Premises, or assign this Lease or permit to any other person to use the Premises.

LEASE CONTINUED

15. Landlord may enter, keys, signs

Landlord may, at reasonable times, enter the Premises to examine, to make repairs or alterations, and to show it to possible buyers, lenders or tenants. Tenant must give to the Landlord a free key to all locks immediately upon any lock change or any request by the Landlord. Locks may not be changed or additional locks installed without Landlord's consent. Doors must be locked at all times. Windows must be locked when the Tenant is away. Landlord may place the usual "For Rent" or "For Sale" signs upon the Premises. Tenant will pay $25.00 for a replacement key from Landlord at the time of the request, and key will be provided within 24 hours.

16. Subordination

This Lease and Tenant's rights are subject and subordinate to all present and future (a) leases for the Premises or the land on which it stands, (b) mortgages on the leases or on the Premises or on the land, (c) agreements securing money paid or to be paid by the lender, under mortgages, and (d) terms, conditions, renewals, changes of any kind in and extensions of the mortgages or leases or Lender agreements. Tenant must promptly execute any certificate(s) that Landlord requests to show that his Lease is subject and subordinate.

17. Condemnation

If all the Premises is taken or condemned by a legal authority, the Term, and Tenant's rights shall end as of the date the authority takes title to the Premises. If any part of the Premises is taken, Landlord may cancel this Lease on notice to Tenant setting forth a cancellation date together with all rent due to that date. The entire award for any taking belongs to Landlord. Tenant gives Landlord any interest Tenant might have to any part of the award and shall make no claim for the value of the remaining part of the Term.

18. Compliance with Authorities

Tenant must, at Tenant's cost, promptly comply with all laws, orders, rules and directions of all governmental authorities, property owners associations, insurance carriers or Board of Fire Underwriters or similar group. Tenant may not do anything that may increase Landlord's insurance premiums. If Tenant does, Tenant must pay the increase as added rent.

19. Tenant's defaults and Landlord's remedies

    A.   Landlord may give 5 days written notice to Tenant to correct any of the following defaults:

       1.   Failure to pay rent or added rent on time.

       2.   Improper assignment of the Lease, improper subletting all or part of the Premises, or allowing another to use the Premises.

       3.   Improper conduct by Tenant or other occupant of the Premises.

       4.   Failure to fully perform any other Term in the Lease.

    B.   If Tenant fails to correct the defaults in section A within the 5 days, Landlord may cancel the Lease by giving Tenant a written three (3) day notice stating the date the Term will end. On that date, the Term and Tenant's rights in this Lease automatically end and Tenant must leave the Premises and give the Landlord the keys. Tenant continues to be responsible for rent, expenses, damages and losses.

    C.   If the Lease is cancelled, or rent or added rent is not paid on time, or Tenant vacated the Premises, Landlord may, in addition to other remedies, take any of the following steps:

       1.   Enter the Premises and remove Tenant and any person or property.

       2.   Use dispossesses eviction or other lawsuit method to take back the Premises.

    D.   If the Lease is ended or Landlord takes back the Premises, rent and added rent for the unexpired Term becomes due and payable. Landlord may re-rent the Premises and anything in it for any term. Landlord may re-rent for a lower rent and give allowances to the new Tenant. Tenant shall be responsible for Landlord's cost of re-renting. Landlord's cost shall include the cost of repairs, decorations, broker's fees, attorney's fees, advertising, and preparation of renting. Tenant shall continue to be responsible for rent, expenses, damages and losses. Any rent received from the re-renting shall be applied to the reduction of money Tenant owes. Tenant waives all rights to return to the Premises after possession is given to the Landlord by a court.

    E.   If "Lead" should be detected in anyone at the dwelling, tenant may (1.) at tenant expense dispose of any lead paint or (2.) move immediately and hold Landlord harmless of legal liability.

20. Bankruptcy

If (1) Tenant assigns property for the benefit of creditors, (2) Tenant files a voluntary petition or an involuntary petition is filed against Tenant under any bankruptcy or insolvency law, or (3) a trustee or receiver of Tenant or Tenant's property is appointed, Landlord may give Tenant thirty (30) days notice of cancellation under the Term of this Lease. If any of the above is not fully dismissed within the 30 days, the Term shall end as of the date stated in the notice. Tenant must continue to pay rent, damages, losses and expenses without the offset.

21. Correcting Tenant's default

If Tenant fails to correct a default after notice from Landlord, Landlord may correct it for Tenant at Tenant's expense. The sum Tenant must repay to Landlord will be added rent.

LEASE CONTINUED

22. Waiver of jury, counterclaim, set off

Landlord and Tenant waive trial by a jury in any matter, which comes up between the parties under or because of this Lease (except for a personal injury or property damage claim). In a proceeding to get possession of the Premises, Tenant shall not have the right to make a counterclaim or set off.

23. Written instructions

Landlord has given and reserves the right to give additional written instructions (if needed) about the care and use of the appliances, equipment and other personal property on the Premises. Tenant must obey the instructions.

24. Broker

There is no Real Estate Broker involved in this Lease.

25. Landlord unable to perform

If due to labor trouble, government order, lack of supply, Tenant's act or neglect, or any other cause not fully within Landlord's reasonable control. Landlord is delayed or unable to (a) carry out any of Landlord's promises or agreements, (b) supply any service to be supplied, (c) make any required repair or changes in the Apartment or Building, or (d) supply any equipment or appliances, this Lease shall not be ended or Tenant's obligations affected.

26. Illegality

If any part of this Lease is not legal, the rest of the Lease will be unaffected.

27. No waiver

Landlord's failure to enforce any terms of this Lease shall not prevent Landlord from enforcing such terms at a later time.

28. Quiet enjoyment

Landlord agrees that if Tenant pays the rent and is not in default under this Lease, Tenant may peaceably and quietly have, hold and enjoy the Premises for the Term of this Lease. Tenant has an expectation of privacy.

29. Successors

This lease is binding on all parties who lawfully succeed to the rights or take the place of the Landlord or Tenant.

30. Representations, changes in Lease

Tenant has read this Lease. All promises made by the Landlord are in this Lease. There are no others. This Lease may be changed only by an agreement in writing signed by and delivered to each party.

31. Paragraph headings

The paragraph headings are for convenience only.

32. Effective date

This Lease is effective when signed by all parties.

33. Written notice

Tenant will give Landlord written notice 60 days before end of Lease if he would like to extend, renew or negotiate this Lease, Landlord will notify Tenant promptly of his Terms or intentions.

34. Check charges

In the event a check is issued that is not covered upon first admission, the Tenant shall be responsible for returned check charges incurred by the Landlord, in addition to the late and administrative charges listed in paragraph 3, and these charges are also added rent.

35. Waterbeds

Tenants may only install waterbeds if they have an insurance policy satisfactory to the Landlord, and with **written** approval from the Landlord.

Lease Continued

36. Taxes and Insurance

Landlord shall be responsible for the following: mortgage payments, property taxes and insurance premiums on the property. Tenant shall be responsible for any insurance, which may be appropriate for his use of the property and his possessions and fully understands that Landlords insurance **does** not cover the Tenant's personal possessions.

37. Association fees and rules

If property is a condo, townhouse, or homeowner's association fees for common elements and amenities are/ are not included in monthly rent, the Tenant agrees to abide by all rules and regulations for the association.

38. Pets

Pets not allowed. If landlord gives written permission tenants agree to keep their pets under control, restrained when outside, not allowed to be unattended for any unreasonable periods, dispose of their pet droppings properly and not to leave food or water outside. Tenants must agree to keep their pet from causing any annoyance or discomfort to others. Tenant will add $200 to their Deposit and requires written permission from the Landlord. This added pet deposit is non-refundable.

39. Illegal drugs

Manufacture, distribution, possession, or use of illegal drugs or a controlled substance at the property is prohibited, and may be cause for immediate eviction.

40. Public assistance

If Tenant presently is a Public Assistance recipient, has not paid a Security Deposit, and later becomes ineligible for assistance, Tenant will immediately provide Landlord with cash Security Deposit equal to one month's rent or vacate the property by the end of that month.

41. Property for sale

This house is not currently for sale. In the event the house is sold during the Term of Lease and the buyer wants possession, Tenant agrees to vacate the property when Landlord gives 60 days written notice. If the house is put up for sale, premises must be available for showing during the following hours; 10 am until 6 pm. Every effort will be made to give 24 hours notice before showing and Tenant agrees to cooperate in showing to prospective buyers.

42. Abandonment

If tenant leaves said premises unoccupied for [A. twenty four (24) consecutive days when rent is paid and not due, or (B. fourteen (14) consecutive days when rent is due and unpaid without notification and approval from the Landlord. These shall be deemed an abandonment and exclude occupant without notice. In such event, owner may dispose of all of tenant's property remaining on said premises by sale or otherwise and use any funds received toward unpaid rent or damages caused by tenant and may re-rent said premises.

43. Legal fees, eviction

If legal action to recover premises is required due to Tenants failure to comply with Terms of this Lease, Landlord will be entitled to reasonable attorney's fees.

44. Representation

Owner has authorization to investigate tenant's credit and employment history and release information about owner's experience with tenant. Also, any statement submitted by tenant in the Application at Rent is to be considered a material inducement to execute this agreement, and the falsifying of any part of such statement shall entitle owner to terminate this agreement immediately, and seek any damages.

45. Authority

The person signing this agreement as the "tenant" states that he or she has the authority to sign for all other persons who will occupy the apartment. All persons listed on this lease are jointly and separately responsible for the full amount or the rent, and all conditions of this lease.

46. Lead Paint

The tenant understands that the property may or may not contain "Lead Paint". The tenant should not move-in if anyone in the family or visitor (regularly 8 hours a day) is now or has ever been diagnosed with elevated levels of "Lead". Upon move in tenant accepts total liability to over see and guard making sure that no child under the age of ten (10) consume particles containing Lead Paint at the property. Tenant agrees to notify the Owner immediately if lead is detected in anyone pertaining to this property.

Lease Continued

FINAL NOTICE: You must not sign, and you must not move in, if any of the conditions in this agreement, or at the property are not satisfactory with you!

Waiver of Attorney Approval. This Lease is not subject to the Tenant's attorney approval. _____
(Tenant's initials)

Waiver of Attorney Approval. This Lease is not subject to the Landlord's attorney approval. _____
(Landlord's initials)

Signatures   The parties have entered into this Lease on the date first above stated.

LANDLORD: TENANT:

_____   _____
                                             «Tenant»

                                             _____
                                             «Tenant_2»

PROPERTY CONDITION REPORT

PROPERTY CONDITION REPORT

Address _____ Apt. # _____
Unit Address _____ Apt. No. _____ Unit Size _____

ITEM	CONDITION

KITCHEN
Doors _____
Walls _____
Ceiling _____
Floors _____
Stove _____
Sink _____
Garbage Disposal _____
Refrigerator _____
Other _____

LIVING ROOM
Doors _____
Walls _____
Ceiling _____
Floors _____
Other _____

BEDROOM # 1
Doors _____
Walls _____
Ceiling _____
Floors _____
Other _____

BEDROOM # 2
Doors _____
Walls _____
Ceiling _____
Floors _____
Other _____

BEDROOM # 3
Doors _____
Walls _____
Ceiling _____
Floors _____
Other _____

BEDROOM # 4
Doors _____
Walls _____
Ceiling _____
Floors _____
Other _____

ITEMS	CONDIITION

ENTERIOR CONDITION
KEYS _____
WINDOWS _____
SCREENS _____
LOCKS _____
VENETIAN BLINDS _____
SHADES _____
DRAPES _____
PORCH & STAIRS _____
HOT WATER HEATER _____

EXTERIOR CONDITION
BUILDING _____
FRONT YARD _____
REAR YARD _____
SIDE YARD _____
OTHER:

FURNACE _____
ELECTRICAL FIXTURES _____
ELECTRICAL OUTLETS _____
AIRCONDITIONING _____

BATHROOM
Doors _____
Walls _____
Ceiling _____
Floors _____
Toilet _____
Tub _____
Shower _____
Other _____

COMMENTS:

ACCEPTANCE:

TENANTS" SIGNATURES: DATES

_____   _____

_____   _____

OWNER   MANAGER   AGENT

_____   _____

_____   _____

COLLECTION RECORD

YEAR _____

Address _____

Tenant _____

Phone # _____

Employer _____

Phone # _____

Rent Amount $ _____

Due on _____ of each month

Amount- Security Deposit $ _____

DATE MOVED IN: _____

DATE MOVED OUT: _____

COMMENTS:

JAN Date		**JUL** Date
Principal		Principal
Late Charge		Late Charge
Total $_____ $_____ $_____		Total $_____ $_____ $_____
FEB Date		**AUG** Date
Principal		Principal
Late Charge		Late Charge
Total $_____ $_____ $_____		Total $_____ $_____ $_____ Date
MAR Date		**SEP** Principal
Principal		Late Charge
Late Charge		Total $_____ $_____ $_____
Total $_____ $_____ $_____		Date
APR Date		**OCT** Principal
Principal		Late Charge
Late Charge		Total $_____ $_____ $_____
Total $_____ $_____ $_____		Date
MAY Date		**NOV** Principal
Principal		Late Charge
Late Charge		Total $_____ $_____ $_____
Total $_____ $_____ $_____		Date
JUN Date		**DEC** Principal
Principal		Late Charge
Late Charge		Total $_____ $_____ $_____
Total $_____ $_____ $_____		

RENTAL AGREEMENT

OWNER: _____   ADRESS: _____

Phone # _____

TENANT: _____

IN CONSIDERATION OF THE TERMS CONTAINED HEREIN, OWNER RENTS THE PROPERTY TO THE TENANT AT:

PROPERTY LOCATION: _____

TERM:
This agreement shall begin _____ and end on _____. Tenant may renew for additional term, **MONTH TO MONTH** thereafter. All other covenants and conditions shall remain in effect for each term. (See "Termination of Agreement" on page 2). AT ANY TIME THIS AGREEMENT CAN BE TERMINATED WITH A 30 DAY NOTICE BY THE TENANT OR THE OWNER WITH NO REASONS NECESSARY OR REQUIRED.

RENT:
Rent shall be $_____ per MONTH (or term), due on the first day of each month. Rent will not be withheld for any reason. The rent can be increased at any time for any reason. All Charges and Expenses that the tenant is responsible for becomes a part of the Rent and is legally collectable immediately.

AGREEMENT AND REMEDIES:
Tenant has inspected the apartment and observed the condition of the property to meet with his/her standard of living. Tenant acknowledges that the property is in good condition and receives it as the same. Tenant agrees to pay for any additional material and/or labor cost (including Lead Paint removal) that he/she feels would improve his/her own living conditions at the property.
I _____ SWEAR THIS DATE _____ IN WRITING THAT "should a dispute arise with the owner that can not be resolved, I will take no other action except that defined under "Termination of Agreement" page 2.

CHARGES:
Tenant will pay a charge of $10.00 if rent is five (5) days late, plus an additional charge of $1.00 for each day thereafter that rent remains unpaid. Tenant will pay $20.00 for an additional key from Owner. Tenant will pay the cost for any and all damage to windows, doors, and locks that he is responsible for.

SECURITY DEPOSIT:
A Security Deposit in the amount of One Months Rent is required, and will be held in trust by the owner until termination of tenancy, and is not to be considered as rent for the last week. The Security Deposit will not be refunded if the tenant vacate the premises with less than one months tenancy. The Security Deposit will be refunded in full within ten (10) days of termination of tenancy (move out), less any damages and cleaning charges, if the tenant has paid at least one months rent.

CARE OF APARTMENT:
Tenant must notify owner in writing within five (5) days of moving in of any items which are damaged or broken. Tenant will not be held responsible for any damage occurring before they moved in. The tenant agrees to pay for damages (including plugged drains) to the apartment that occur during his/her term only. Broken glass of windows shall be replaced by tenant. The tenant agrees not to paint or make any alterations to the property without written permission from the owner. The tenant is responsible for, and shall take care of the apartment during their occupancy and agrees to keep the property clean inside and outside. The tenant is responsible to replace Smoke Detector Batteries. The tenant will maintain the premises (including hallways, stairs, windows, doors, garage, yard, etc.) in a reasonable and habitable condition, and remove any particles that contain Lead Paint. The tenant will be responsible for snow removal, lawn mowing, leaves, garbage containers, and removal of any garbage or debris accumulated at the premises. On the morning of, or the night before pickup, garbage will be sit on the curb and properly bundled by the tenant. The tenant will pay for all Garbage Code Violations. After the first 60 day period the tenant will be responsible for Roach, Insect, and Rat Extermination. THE TENANT WILL NOT ALLOW ANY KIND OF " INSPECTION" (BY ANYONE) AT THE PROPERTY WITHOUT THE OWNERS PERMISSION.

RENTAL AGREEMENT CONTINUED

RETURNED CHECKS: A $30.00 charge will be due for each check returned by a bank. In the event of bank errors, there will be no such charge provided owner receives the bank's written acknowledgment of such error.

TRANSFER OR SUBLETTING: The tenant agrees that he/she will not transfer or sublet this property, or any part of it, without the written consent of the owner.

VISITORS: Tenant will be responsible for all damage, acts, and conduct of any visitor they permit onto the property

TERMINATION OF AGREEMENT: a. **Release Clause**: The tenant must give a thirty (30) day written notice of his/her intention to move. Notice should be mailed to owner at address on page 1, and must correspond to the agreement period on page 1. Should "Lead Paint" be detected in anyone at the dwelling, tenant may leave immediately.

b. **Notice to Vacate**: Owner may request tenant to vacate the premises immediately with a written notice any time when either rent is not paid (None Payment) or damage is being done. Owner may give A thirty (30) day written notice for any other reason (Any Grounds), no reason required. The thirty day notice must correspond to the agreement period on page 1. If tenant fails to vacate, any Personal Property left on the premises can be "thrown out" or "sold", and the proceeds applied toward any damages, rent, late charges, court cost, marshal's fee, moving, storage and/or any other expenses.

USE OF PREMISES: The tenant shall use his/her apartment as private living quarters for ____ adults, ____ children, and for no other purpose whatsoever.

Tenant may not allow any additional person to occupy the apartment without written approval from the owner. If owner approves in writing, a sum of not more that $75.00 a month shall be due for each additional occupant, except newly born children of the tenant. No unauthorized vehicles permitted. The tenant is responsible to notify the Owner of "inoperable" or "missing" Smoke Detectors.

Tenant agrees not to use the apartment for business purposes. The tenant shall not violate any regulation of the Board of Health, Fire Underwriters, City Ordinance and Codes, or State or Federal Laws of any nature, and shall not use the apartment for any unlawful or immoral purposes. If probable cause exist for the issuance of a search warrant at the premises, whether or not narcotics or contraband are actually seized, the damage that occurs as a result of this warrant shall be the liability of the tenant.

Tenant agrees not to use a "Water Bed" or a "Clothes Washer Machine" without permission of the Owner. These items demand special handling, complete analysis, and requires an additional charge.

Fortification of the premises is prohibited. Fortification includes, but is not limited to, the installation of steel doors, barricaded doors, windows and doors boarded and secured, but having small openings, slits or peepholes consistent with those used to pass money and narcotics.

Use of the premises for the possession, sale, or distribution of narcotics or marijuana is in violation of articles 220 and 221 of the penal law. For any of the behaviors listed above the tenant must "quit the premises" immediately upon the demand.

CLEANING CHARGES: Tenant will leave apartment clean at the end of this tenancy. Tenant will place all unwanted items in bags or boxes, and remove same from the apartment, and place at the curb on refuse collection pickup day. A cleaning fee will be charged if the tenant fails to clean the apartment or dispose of the trash.

PETS: Tenant agree that **no animal**, dog, cat, bird, snake, or pet of any kind may be kept on said premises.

RIGHT OF ENTRY: The owner or agent may enter at any reasonable time to inspect, repair, maintain, or show the premises

Page 2

Rental Agreement continued

COLLECTION AND EVICTION COST: In the event it becomes necessary for the owner to take legal action or employ an Attorney to enforce any of owner's rights under this agreement or any law of this State, tenant agrees to pay owner the actual amount of all cost, expenses, and Attorney's fees incurred by owner in connection therewith, whether or not a law suit is actually filed.

UTILITIES: Tenant agree to pay for all Gas, Water, Heat, and Electricity that he uses. Tenant agrees to "hold harmless" the Owner, and to pay all these bills immediately when they become due.

REPAIRS: Tenant must immediately notify the owner of plumbing leaks, failure of heating or hot water systems, and electrical malfunctions. Those items not caused by the tenant will be repaired by the owner within a reasonable time period (5 days). Tenant is liable for all other repairs (including rat & roach control).

INSURANCE: The owner's insurance policy covers damage or loss by fire and theft to the building and owner's furnishings only. The owner shall not be responsible for loss, injury or damage to the personal property of the tenant, his guest, or visitors, caused directly or indirectly by acts of God, fire, theft, burglary, malicious acts, riots, civil commotion, the elements, defects in the building, furnishings, equipment, walks or landscaping, or by neglect of other residents, or owners of adjacent property. Tenant agrees to make no claims against owner for any such damage of loss. Tenant agrees to pay for damage, and/or get a Police Report for any damage done to the property by others (A claim may need to be filed with an insurance company).

ABANDONMENT If tenant leaves said premises unoccupied for {A-eighteen (18) consecutive days when rent is paid and not due, or {B-seven (7) consecutive days when rent is due and unpaid; -it shall be deemed an abandonment and exclude occupant without notice. In such event, owner may dispose of all of tenant's property remaining on said premises by sale or otherwise and use any funds received toward unpaid rent or damages caused by tenant and may re-rent said premises.

REPRESENTATION Owner has authorization to investigate tenant's credit and employment history and release information about owner's experience with tenant. Also, any statement submitted by tenant in the Application to Rent is to be considered a material inducement to execute this agreement, and the falsifying of any part of such statement shall entitle owner to terminate this agreement immediately, and seek any damages..

AUTHORITY: The person signing this agreement as the "tenant" states that he or she has the authority to sign and is the person who will occupy the apartment.

LEAD PAINT The tenant understands that the property may contain "Lead Paint"! The tenant should not move-in if anyone "in the family" or "visitor (regularly 8 hours a day)" is now or has ever been diagnosed with elevated levels of "Lead". Tenant accepts total liablility to oversee and guard, making sure that no child under the age of ten (10) consume particles containing Lead Paint at the property. Tenant agrees to notify the Owner immediately if lead is detected in anyone pertaining to this property.

I APPROVE THIS PROPERTY TO BE IN GOOD CONDITION. I AGREE TO GIVE PROPER NOTICE AND VACATE THE PREMISES IF SOMEONE IS "DIAGNOSED WITH LEAD PAINT OR IF THE "CONDITIONS BECOME UNSUITABLE" FOR ANY REASONS. I HAVE READ ALL THREE (3) PAGES AND EXCEPT ALL TERMS OF THIS AGREEMENT.

SIGNATURE: _____   DATE: _____

FINAL NOTICE: You must not sign, and you must not move in, if any of the conditions in this agreement, or at the property are not satisfactory with you!

Page 3

PROMISE LETTER

At this time I am renting _____ from
_____ the Owner. I realize that I am $ _____
behind in my rent at this time, and that amount should have been paid on
_____.

**I promise that I will pay the above amount owed by the ____ day of
_____, 20_____.**

In the event that I for any reason do not follow through with the above promise, I shall vacate my apartment immediately, and no later than the above mention date. If I fail to do this, I give my permission to said owner to <u>change the locks</u> on my door and allow him to <u>re-rent my apartment</u>. If the apartment I am renting is unfurnished, I give said owner or agent my permission to remove the furniture from my apartment and set it out on the street.

The owner will return all personal clothing and belongings to me. I realize it is my responsibility to pick up my personal belongings and articles no later than 48 hours after the locks on my apartment have been changed.

_____
Date

_____
Signature of Tenant

3 Day Notice

"3 DAY NOTICE TO PAY OR QUIT"

<u>   </u>
Date

TO: _____

_____

_____

Dear _____ .

Please be advised that the owner of the property listed above has elected to <u>terminate your tenancy</u> because of **"your non-payment of rent"**! ! !

The term of this Notice expires on mid-night, _____ ____, 20 _____.
                                         Date

You can consider this as the written and <u>final notice for you to vacate</u>.

In the event of your failure to vacate the said premises within such period as listed above you will be deemed guilty of an unlawful detainer and legal action will be initiated against you for restitution of the premises and for the damages assessed against you in accordance with the provision of the unlawful detainer law. Also be advised that you will be required to pay any legal fees incurred after this period of time.

Please call me at _____ for definite arrangements!

Sincerely,

_____
Owner

PERSONAL AND CONFINDENTIAL

30 DAY NOTICE

"30 DAY NOTICE"

Date: _____

TO: _____
_____
_____

Dear _____,

Please be advised that the owner of the property listed above has elected to **"terminate your tenancy"** under the terms of the Rental Agreement. Your term expires on mid-night, _____. This is the final **"written notice"** admonishing you to vacate, as required by the Rental Agreement. After this date you are designated as **"HOLD OVER".**

In the event of your failure to vacate the said premises within such period as listed above, you will be deemed guilty of an unlawful detainer and legal action will be initiated against you for restitution of said premises and for damages assessed against you in accordance with the provisions of the unlawful detainer law. Also be advised that you will be required to pay any "legal Fees" incurred after this thirty day period. See your "Rental Agreement" for details.

Should you move by _____, there will be no rent due for the following month. Please call me if there are any questions.

Sincerely,

Owner _____

Phone # _____

PERSONAL AND CONFIDENTIAL . . . .

Introductory Letter

INTRODUCTORY LETTER

TO: _____   Date _____

_____

_____

Dear _____,

    You are hereby notified that the undersigned has purchased the building at
_____. Please fill out the enclosed forms
for my records and return them to me within the next three days. I will contact
you soon regarding the rental arrangements.

    Any rent due for your apartment at present should be mailed to me at:

_____

_____

_____

    If you have any questions, you may call me at phone number

_____

Sincerely,

_____

CERTIFICATE OF ACHIEVEMENT

AWARDED TO

_____

For Completion on the Course::
"COLLECTION STRATEGIES"
for the Real Estate Owner

Awarded this _____ day of _____, 20____

Eula C. Dozier
Eula C. Dozier, Author & Instructor

www.ingramcontent.com/pod-product-compliance
Lightning Source LLC
Chambersburg PA
CBHW052245290526
45785CB00016B/1314